An Intellectual History of Liberalism

NEW FRENCH THOUGHT

SERIES EDITORS
Thomas Pavel and Mark Lilla

TITLES IN THE SERIES

Mark Lilla, ed., *New French Thought: Political Philosophy*

Gilles Lipovetsky, *The Empire of Fashion: Dressing Modern Democracy*

Pierre Manent, *An Intellectual History of Liberalism*

Jacques Bouveresse, *Wittgenstein Reads Freud: The Myth of the Unconscious*

Blandine Kriegel, *The State and the Rule of Law*

FORTHCOMING TITLES

Alain Renaut, *The Age of the Individual: A History of Modern Subjectivity*

Marcel Gauchet, *The Disenchantment of the World*

Pierre Manent

An Intellectual History
of Liberalism

Translated by Rebecca Balinski

With a Foreword by Jerrold Seigel

 NEW FRENCH THOUGHT

PRINCETON UNIVERSITY PRESS · PRINCETON, NEW JERSEY

Copyright © 1995 by Princeton University Press
Published by Princeton University Press, 41 William Street,
Princeton, New Jersey 08540
In the United Kingdom: Princeton University Press, Chichester, West Sussex

Translated from the French edition of Pierre Manent, *Histoire intellectuelle du libéralisme:
Dix leçons* (Paris: Calmann-Lévy, 1987)

Library of Congress Cataloging-in-Publication Data

Manent, Pierre.
[Histoire intellectuelle du libéralisme. English]
An intellectual history of liberalism / Pierre Manent ; translated by Rebecca Balinski ; with
a foreword by Jerrold Seigel.
p.   cm. — (New French thought)
Includes bibliographical references and index.
ISBN 0-691-03437-0 (cl.)
ISBN 0-691-02911-3 (pbk.)
1. Liberalism—History.   I. Title   II. Series.
JC571.M326613   1994
320.5′12′09—dc20   94-3110

Published with the assistance of the French Ministry of Culture

This book has been composed in Sabon and Bauer Bodoni

Princeton University Press books are printed on acid-free paper and meet the guidelines
for permanence and durability of the Committee on Production Guidelines for Book
Longevity of the Council on Library Resources

Third printing, and first paperback printing, 1996

Printed in the United States of America by Princeton Academic Press

10   9   8   7   6   5   4   3

Contents

READERS PICKING up a book that offers an account of the history of liberal thought in just ten short chapters may suppose they are in the presence of a kind of primer, a handy introduction that puts complexity aside until later—if later ever comes. In several ways Pierre Manent's work will seem to satisfy such expectations. It is written in simple, direct language; it bears no heavy weight of footnotes or scholarly apparatus; and it moves gracefully from one highpoint to another, along the way bravely providing concise summaries of complex subjects—for example, the history of relations between Church and state over several centuries of European history—in a few smooth and unblinking paragraphs. Those who do not know the subject well will come away from reading the book having encountered much of the basic substance of political thinking between Machiavelli in the sixteenth century and Tocqueville in the nineteenth.

Its resemblance to a primary textbook ends there, however. Behind a facade of simplicity, Manent has constructed a sophisticated, pointed, argumentative, sometimes brilliant and often controversial account of the nature of modern political life, considered from the point of view of the assumptions and presuppositions that shape and inspire it. Although he approaches liberalism as a body of political theory or reflection, through the eight thinkers to whom major chapters are dedicated, the author's real quarry is not political thought but political life, and the liberalism he has in his sights is not one particular and delimited attitude toward modern politics but the world of assumptions and experiences within which we all move and act. The "intellectual history of liberalism" recounted here is, as he says, a "scale model" of the political history of Europe, and the story of past theorists becomes—to recall a phrase from a well-known French thinker of a very different stamp—a "history of the present."

Manent's project, then, is to discover the outlines of present political life within the lineaments of past political thought; his way of finding the link between those two levels may also surprise American and English readers. As good pragmatists or utilitarians—when we are not more-or-less-good Marxists—we may assume that ideas exist in service of real, practical conditions and interests, and that a history of theory becomes a history of events and institutions when it sees through the ideas to the more substantial and material situations out of which they arise. Here things take place

quite differently. Pierre Manent believes that the content of modern liberalism derives from a fundamental orientation toward politics chosen by
early-modern Europeans in order to free themselves from the intellectual
and spiritual influence of the Catholic Church; that adopting this orientation required the theoretical materials provided by the founders of
liberalism—in his account, Machiavelli, Hobbes, and Locke; that the later
evolution of liberal theory and practice can be understood as the working-
out of the consequences of this original choice; and that the political frustrations of our own day still derive from the powerful dilemmas created when
our progenitors took up this liberal stance three or four centuries ago.

The stance in question is a negative one, the denial that political life
serves a higher purpose: we moderns, though still in our way the political
animals Aristotle long ago defined us to be, do not enter into relations with
others in order to realize some good or end inherent in human nature.
Classical thinkers assumed that human beings—like every form of existence ranged within the organized cosmos—possessed such goods or ends
and that every particular political arrangement or action could be judged
according to how well it corresponded to them. This was one feature of
classical theory that recommended it to Christians and, notably, to many
scholastic thinkers and that made the medieval and Renaissance rediscovery of the classical heritage an insufficient basis for setting politics on
purely secular foundations, since any admission that a higher end existed
could be seized on by the Church as a license to judge secular life by
religious standards. Hence the radical rupture constituted by Machiavelli's
uncompromising location of politics within a sphere from which all moral
judgment was excluded, and later by Hobbes's justification of sovereignty
by way of an image of human beings as naturally drawn to others only in
order to achieve domination over them. Machiavelli and Hobbes set the
terms for the modern definition of the subject and object of political action
as the pure, bare individual of the state of nature, void of any goal outside
the narrow confines of the self.

Such an orientation toward politics derived law from the needs of a
human nature deprived of any positive qualities that might give it a larger
purpose; at the same time it exalted the state as the only means that could
assure the survival and existence of the morally impoverished individuals
its orientation presupposed. The "rights" it might attribute to these individuals could never succeed in rooting the justification of state power in
the needs of human nature, because the state had always to be conceived
and legitimated as the organ that prevented any particular purpose from
realizing itself in social life. (Rousseau would proffer a particularly ingenious solution to this dilemma, but he only succeeded in shifting the
ground on which it had to be confronted.) Liberal politics thus vacillates

between exalting the state and defending against it, while simultaneously alternating between idealized and demonized visions of society and human nature. Law and nature, politics and society, shift back and forth between a phase in which each looks to the other to furnish what it itself lacks, and an opposing moment wherein each devotes its resources to restraining the power of the other. "State" and "civil society" have each had their moments of unchecked independence, sometimes with destructive and tragic results, but in the end the suppressed pole has always reemerged to contest the temporary domination of its simultaneously desired and suspected partner. Thus do we live still with the consequences of the original choice that established individuals as the only basis of social and political life, still turning in the empty space our forefathers hollowed out for us as if centuries later—Manent concludes—"nothing had happened."

Although Manent's account of liberalism is critical, I think readers will see that it is also sympathetic—not to the philosophical and ethical presuppositions of liberal politics perhaps, but to the situation, the hopes and frustrations, of those (and that includes most of us) for whom its moral interior constitutes an inescapable life-world. This combination of criticism and sympathy, skeptical about modern politics but disabused of the *marxisant* enthusiasms of a Sartre and impermeable to the Nietzschean paradoxes of a Foucault, provides one reason why Mark Lilla and Thomas Pavel have chosen the current book to represent what they call "New French Thought." Manent illustrates very well one direction taken by the vigorous reflection on the nature of liberal society that has developed in France since the middle of the 1970s, together with the rapprochement between French and "Anglo-Saxon" philosophy that has been interwoven with it.[1] In Manent's case, the particular "Anglo-Saxon" brand of thinking that has colored his reflections most is that of Leo Strauss—not "Anglo-Saxon" at all, to be sure, but given a home in America and imported from there into France. Manent exemplifies the intellectual vitality that recent French scholars and thinkers have been able to draw from their encounters with Anglophone traditions. Readers may still recognize a certain "Frenchness" to his work in a style of presentation that gives form to analysis in deft and rapid *aperçus* as often as in sustained theoretical elaboration, and will perhaps even find an echo of the Sartrian image of man as "a useless passion" in the antinomies of modern politics developed in the book's last few pages. What is most characteristic of Manent's intellectual stance, however, is his attempt to draw the history of liberalism out of one original moral and intellectual choice, to discover behind particular and characteristic manifestations of modern politics the general and defining attitude that formed it in the first place and that has never ceased to shape it.

Consider, for instance, his understanding of the idea of the state of nature as providing both an image of human beings over whom no traditional claims to authority have any legitimate power, yet also a basis for setting up an incontestable obligation to political obedience. Such a notion, developed in order to combat the power of religious doctrine without undermining social stability, cuts people off from every social attachment while delivering them over to the agency—the state—that establishes social life in a form that excludes any partial or specific social good. Liberal thinkers were still wrestling with the consequences of this set of moves in the age of Benjamin Constant and Tocqueville. Or take his related argument that Lockean theory gave an opening to a strong executive power in an almost "Hobbesian" way, despite Locke's attempt to limit royal authority. This situation developed because the legislative power, theoretically supreme by virtue of its ability to represent society's various and different interest, could not embody the singlemindedness, the unity of will and action required to give practical stability to political society. Thus the strength of modern executives in England and America derives from the exigencies of modern politics, not from the survival of older monarchical assumptions.

But it is his account of liberal theory and practice in the age of Montesquieu, Rousseau, and the French Revolution that shows the method in operation at its most stimulating and challenging. In Manent's reading, what is most significant about Montesquieu's account of the balance of power is that its implications extend from the state to society; both become realms of negative freedom where strength and weakness feed on one another. The executive and legislative powers that restrain each other in the strictly political realm are represented in the social sphere by parties to which people give allegiance, but only provisionally, since each serves the purpose of liberty only so long as it cannot achieve the domination it denies the other. The life of the state expands, but its ability to act in society contracts, and this limitation serves to make the private realms of wealth and culture more satisfying than participation in political life. But the liberty individuals find there is negative too; each must renounce over others the power he fears they may gain over himself. The inhabitants of such a society will find it alternatively liberating and constricting; their satisfactions and frustrations combine to inspire them with visions of an ideal state, but they will never be able to bring any transformative project to realization, because modern politics is designed to frustrate every such definite purpose. In the end such people find themselves divided between their political and social lives, between existence as "citizen," and as "man"—just the condition to which Rousseau will respond.

Rousseau was not just a critic of absolutism, but equally of the society that replaced it, at once the successor of Hobbes and of Montesquieu. It was the nature of the society to which sovereign power brought social peace that troubled him so much, the society of *amour-propre* where people were divided within themselves by the need to be constantly comparing themselves with their fellows, able to be aware of themselves only in relation to others, but drawn outside themselves only by the promptings of egotism. In order to heal this division, Rousseau evolved a new notion of the state of nature, within which he was able to grant wholeness to individuals, but only at the price of denying them sociability. The task was to bring the two qualities together, to unify human beings with themselves, but inside the social state. Rousseau achieved this by basing the social contract on his novel notion of freedom as self-legislation, the human ability to follow laws of humanity's own making. People who lived under such self-imposed laws would recover the wholeness of their original natural lives, but only at the cost of repressing every expression of the personal interest that was revealed as their second nature within existing society. Thus political society had to put itself on a new basis by at once fulfilling nature and repressing it; it had to impose on men the unity they had willingly given up, return them to nature by denaturing them. The contradictions in these ideas are inescapable because they correspond to those of human nature, forever divided between animality and liberty.

Rousseau achieved just what liberalism had previously found impossible: justifying sovereignty on the basis of bare individual nature by his novel attribution to individuals of an innate capacity for self-legislative freedom. But the result was to make the earlier liberal notion of freedom as security pale beside this much more vital and powerful idea of autonomy. The cost of finding an innate end or good within the pure individuality on which liberalism had sought to construct a politics of neutrality was to release in society the demand that autonomy replace the narrow liberty of liberalism, and this meant a call for revolution. Modern politics can recover a unified purpose only by revolutionizing itself, by imposing from above, but in the name of society, the unity that can free human nature from itself.

I will not continue this summary of Manent's argument through the remaining chapters on the Revolution and the transformed liberalism of the nineteenth century, although I think readers will find his accounts of Benjamin Constant's politics of irony and of Alexis de Tocqueville's picture of democracy as a way of life engaged in a perpetual search for itself among the most stimulating and original parts of the book. Instead let me close by raising a few questions that Manent's imaginative account of liberalism calls up in the mind of one American who practices a less philosophical and more prosaic mode of intellectual history.

The first of these concerns the founding impulse behind liberal politics. Manent locates this impulse in the revolt against religious authority and makes the liberal exclusion of particular goods or ends from the realm of the state appear as a consequence of the way secular politicians like Machiavelli and Hobbes banished every independent moral goal or purpose from politics. Such a view resonates with many elements of early liberalism, but it asks us to conceive it first as an act of aggression toward a religious culture whose danger to secular values arose from its power and intactness, so that the only way to combat it was by frontal assault. The rise of liberalism could be just as well, if not better, described in just the opposite terms—as a response to a religious culture whose internal dissolution constituted a grave threat to European life. Machiavelli appears in Manent's story, but Luther does not. Yet the growth of state power in the early modern period owed at least as much to the progress of the Reformation as it did to Machiavelli's maxims and precepts, and the same should be said about the erosion of belief that political life could be oriented toward commonly acknowledged higher goods or ends. Recent studies suggest that one main reason for the attempt to base politics on theories of natural law in the sixteenth and seventeenth centuries lay in the need to find a foundation that could withstand the crumbling of religious unity.[2]

What gives this historical observation a certain theoretical weight is that it returns liberalism's origins to the ground of pluralism, whose affirmation in the guise of tolerance has a place in traditional histories of liberalism that becomes much less significant in Manent's account. Manent asks us to derive liberal pluralism from the Hobbesian reduction of politics to power and fear, but his own account of Hobbes reminds us that in seventeenth-century England things went the other way around: it was the impossibility of achieving any common religious orientation that made it necessary to establish politics on some other basis. Here I think we arrive at one of the ways in which Manent's history reflects its French pedigree, placing liberalism in a context where its principles served as intellectual projectiles in a campaign against the authority of a still-powerful old regime, rather than as bricks to build a new structure required by that regime's already palpable dissolution. Manent rereads the history of liberalism in a way that parallels his colleague François Furet's rereading of the Revolution. He attributes the dilemmas of modern politics to the problematic nature of attempting to replace one holistic form of sovereignty with another, rather than (as in an earlier historiography) to the conflicts engendered by the decline of old powers and the need to reconcile competing social interests.[3]

In other words, Manent's attempt to secure a rapprochement between Hobbes and Locke makes visible some things that conventional histories of liberalism have obscured, but at the cost of collapsing the distinction between liberalism and the authoritarian potentials that grew up alongside it—precisely the distinction that the traditional separation between the two great English theorists serves to maintain. A liberal lineage that makes Machiavelli and Hobbes the family's founders is bound to produce a different legacy than one that attributes paternity to Locke. But I suspect the root of the problem lies earlier, in the link Manent seeks to establish between Machiavelli and Hobbes. Against the attempt to join them together as expressions of a single political and philosophical impulse, one might suggest that what makes both characteristically modern is that each responded to a different kind of modern political crisis. Machiavelli's often shocking maxims and recommendations reflected a desperate desire to put back together the humpty-dumpty of Italian political life after the great fall imposed by the wars that followed the French invasion of 1494,[4] whereas Hobbes's theory was a response to the internal collapse of English religious and political unity during the 1640s. Both of these situations—foreign domination and civil war—are capable of snapping the links that bind individuals together and of engendering the desire for a strong power to reknit the patches of national life. To argue from these two situations that modern politics begins from the rejection of all values that lie beyond the individual, and then that such a politics necessarily opens the way to dictatorship because it locates the source of law outside the individuals who are imagined to be its basis, requires a certain historical sleight of hand, delegitimating certain features of modern culture and politics and creating nostalgia for a world that remains—and probably should remain—beyond recall.

An alternative to Manent's perspective, then, would regard liberal theory and practice not as themselves the powers that eliminated higher goods and ends from modern politics, but as responses—as much restorative and reconstructive as rebellious—to conditions and developments that were already undermining classical and Christian assumptions. Among these conditions and developments were not only religious division, but also the rise of science and of market economies (both of which appear in Manent's story in challenging ways that it is better to let readers discover for themselves). The society and culture based on modern science and economic productivity creates a "background picture" with no space for moral sources outside the self, casting upon the people who aspire toward it the task of giving meaning to individual and social life.[5] This is not the place to suggest in what ways the figures treated in this book might be seen differently from such a viewpoint, since my goal is instead to recommend the very stimulating and bracing readings proffered by Pierre Manent. I think readers will agree with me in finding the encounter with them eminently worthwhile, inviting us to a new and enlivening reconsideration of the cultural and political matrix that gave—and still gives—form to modern life.

Jerrold Seigel

M Y INTENTION in this essay is to present the main themes and the decisive moments of the history of liberalism. For almost three centuries this political doctrine constituted the principal current of modern politics in Europe and the West. Thus I have felt it necessary to begin by sketching out an interpretation of European history prior to liberalism, so as to make the development of liberalism itself intelligible. The reader will not find a political history of Europe in these pages, but rather a scale model of this history, a summary of its major articulations. For guides, I have taken some of the principal works of political philosophy, from Machiavelli to Tocqueville. It is, in my view, the history of political philosophy that sheds the most light on the unfolding of our history and on the nature of our political regimes.

A singular feature of the present historical situation is that political thought and political life are, in modern times, intimately linked. This is something new. The political history of Greece or Rome can be related without referring to "ideas" or "doctrines." In his work on the Peloponnesian War, Thucydides does not devote a single page to what we would call the "intellectual" or "cultural" life of the period. Yet, still today, his history is considered the masterpiece of Greek historiography, perhaps of all historiography. This fact is all the more remarkable since Greece was the birthplace of philosophy, and in particular of political philosophy. It was from the experience of life in the Greek city-state that Plato and Aristotle elaborated their interpretations of human life, which constitute the matrix of all subsequent philosophy. But these interpretations emerged *after* the great cycle of Greek politics occurred. The case of modern political philosophy is completely different. One is tempted to say that it was conceived and chosen *before* being implemented. It was at dawn that the owl of liberalism took flight.

For what did these modern written "constitutions" and the "declarations of rights" proclaimed to establish their "freedom" suggest, if not an emancipation of the "idea," a rise in the political power of the "theory"? The American Founding Fathers were as concerned about interpreting Montesquieu's thought and benefiting from his authority as socialists later were about understanding what Marx "really said." As Hamilton wrote in the first of *The Federalist* papers in 1787, Americans have the responsibility of deciding before the world if it is possible to found a good government "from reflection and choice," or if humanity is forever condemned to be the plaything of "accident and force." In a word, there is in liberal politics something essentially deliberate and experimental, that implies a conscious and "constructed" plan.

It will be said that such an approach clarifies nothing. Either it is trivial—every human action, other than reflexes or passion, implies deliberation—or it assumes that "ideas rule the world." That this approach is not trivial, that it does not assume that "ideas rule the world" (whatever that means) can be demonstrated by an example.

One of the principal "ideas" of liberalism, as we know, is that of the "individual." The individual is that being who, because he is human, is naturally entitled to "rights" that can be enumerated, rights that are attributed to him independently of his function or place in society and that make him the equal of any other man. As familiar as this idea may seem, it really ought to strike us as strange. How can rights be attributed to the individual as individual if rights govern relationships between several individuals, if the very idea of a right presupposes an already instituted community or society? How can political legitimacy be founded on the rights of the individual, if he never exists as such, if he is always necessarily linked to other individuals, to a family, class, profession, or nation? However, it is on this idea, so obviously "asocial" and "apolitical," that the liberal body politic was progressively constructed. What is an election with universal suffrage, if not that moment when each person strips himself of his social or natural characteristics—income, profession, even sex—to become a "simple individual"? It is that moment when the body politic peacefully breaks up, becoming a "state of nature," only to reconstruct itself immediately afterward. Nor is there any doubt that this individual, so obviously "imaginary," has tended more and more to become reality. The inhabitants of Western democracies have become ever more autonomous, ever more equal, and have felt themselves progressively less defined by the family or social class to which they belong.

Observing such a power—not of ideas in general, but of this particular idea—we are led to two questions. First, how did the idea of the individual initiate and guide our political development? And, second, how and why was it born? Other questions flow from these. Why, in societies where this idea was unknown, did philosophers elaborate it? What were the problems that led Europeans to conceive of such an original idea? As long as we fail to respond to these questions, Europe's history remains as sealed to us as that of vanished empires.

Some will say that these questions have already been answered. It is true that no epoch has been more studied than the modern centuries I am going to cover, none has given rise to so many interpretations. A vast number of historians, sociologists, and philosophers have endeavored to make the originality of European political development intelligible. I, too, believe that everything has been said and that everything is known. I shall not be presenting any event that is not already well known, nor commenting on any text that does not already have its honored place in the history of ideas. I simply shall be trying to suggest that this remarkable history is not our past; it is our present. Not only are our roots in it, not only does it pervade our memory. Our present political regime remains determined, in its generating principle, by this origin. Its singularity still dwells in us because we continue to feel the consequences of the solemn decisions taken three centuries ago.

It is widely believed that the originality of European political history stems from Christianity, and that the development of modern politics can be described as a process of "secularization." What are liberty and equality, after all, if not "biblical values" shaping civic life? The thesis was born and acquired its credence just after the French Revolution. It had the merit of reconciling proponents and opponents of the "new freedom": there were those who thought that the hour of human maturity had arrived and those who remained attached to the old religion. The former saw in Christianity the first expression of human liberty and equality, hidden under the veils of grace or hampered by the swaddling clothes of alienation. The latter celebrated modern freedom as the last conquest of the Gospel. We must remember, however, that this reconciliation (which in France took more than a century to be achieved) came about just after the Christian religion had been totally stripped of all political power for the first time, power that it would never regain. Perhaps the lassitude of battle had weakened the conquerors as much as the conquered. In any case the principles of the new politics—the rights of man and citizen, freedom of conscience, sovereignty of the people—had been forged during the two previous centuries in a bitter fight against Christianity, and particularly against the Catholic Church. The decisive question then is the following: must the Enlightenment's war against Christianity be seen as the expression of an immense misunderstanding, for which we must seek to grasp the "historical reasons"? Or does this period give us the meaning of the modern political venture, and thus of liberalism, much more clearly than the subsequent period of reconciliation?

Such an alternative will be unacceptable to most historians. Admitting the second hypothesis would be tantamount to confirming the point of view of the historical actors themselves, deliberately ignoring what the Enlightenment and Christianity allegedly had in common. As for the first, it can be retorted that the Enlightenment's battle was not directed against Christianity as such, against Christian opinion, but against religion's political power. Thus there is an intelligible continuity between two historical phases: the first led the fight against this opinion's political power, the second recognized this opinion as legitimate *as opinion,* and even attributed an eminent value to it.

These objections are plausible and sound impartial. However, nothing guarantees that this disjunction between power and opinion, which we take for granted and which our regimes reflect, is founded in nature; it may simply be the founding prejudice or particular opinion of our regimes. As soon as the least doubt on this point assails us, the relationship between the two phases of our history appears in a new light.

It was because the challenge presented came from a particular opinion, Christianity, that the liberal disjunction between power (in general) and opinion (in general) occurred. Did the world have to wait for Christianity, so that, by opposing it, we could finally reach our natural equilibrium? Perhaps instead it is possible that the means invented to confront this challenge—those means that became our political regime—retain traces of the accident that gave them birth. And, further, perhaps those means in turn become strangely problematic once the original problem has been resolved to general satisfaction. Does the "indeterminacy" credited to our political regimes mean that we are seeing explicitly instituted the disjunction between power, knowledge, and right that is essential to freedom? Or does it rather bring to light the paradox of a state which, having wished to close itself off from Christianity's power, from the power of one particular opinion, is endlessly obliged to deprive any opinion of power?

I have tried to treat these matters to the best of my ability. That means that I did not try to pit myself against the great works that have already clarified them. I have only risked a raid between standing armies, in the hope that the speed of my advance might protect me from their objections without depriving me of their knowledge.

An Intellectual History of Liberalism

CHAPTER I

Europe and the
Theologico-Political Problem

HOW SHALL we begin? Where do we begin? The period preceding the establishment of liberal regimes is conventionally called the ancien régime—an entirely retrospective or negative designation to which another, positive or prospective one is bound to be preferable. This might be called the era of "absolute" or "national" monarchies. It is the notion of *sovereignty* that gives form to the latter. As it prevailed in Europe, this notion was radically new in history. To understand it, we have to understand the world from which it emerged and the world it then reorganized. In short, however intimidating the task, we must take a prospective view of European history—more precisely of the *problem* of European history—from the fall of the Roman Empire.

What were the political forms at men's disposal after this event? "At their disposal" does not mean that these forms were already fully constituted; on the contrary, it was a time of general disintegration. But they were present in men's consciousness as significant, and perhaps desirable, political possibilities.

The first form was obviously the *empire,* which had collapsed in the West but remained in the East. It is impossible to overemphasize just how powerful the idea of empire was in men's minds, even long after the Roman Empire had fallen. Every king wanted to be "emperor in his kingdom." The Holy Roman Empire died officially only in 1806, and was followed by two Napoleonic Empires, Bismarck's Reich, and the Third Reich. Even today people still speak of the idea of the "World State." What is the content of the idea of empire? It is the bringing together of all the known world, of the *orbis terrarum,* under a unique power. The idea of empire does not refer primarily to the conquering zeal of a few individuals (Alexander, Caesar, Charlemagne, or Napoleon). It corresponds instead to men's unity, to the universality of human nature, which wants to be recognized and addressed by a unique power. It is a *natural* political idea.

The *city-state* was the other significant model. A city-state is potentially present from the moment a sufficient number of men are assembled in one place. Like the empire, this type of political organization enjoyed great prestige, a reflection of the Roman Republic's glory (and also, through Rome, of the glory of Athens and Sparta). This prestige remained considerable in Europe wherever certain city-states reached a high degree of political power, economic prosperity, or intellectual eminence: the Hanseatic towns, Venice, or Florence for example. In decline after the monarchies' triumph, it returned to nourish hopes for a new civic life, for "freedom" (though within a national framework, which changed profoundly the original idea). The idea of the city-state implies a public space where citizens deliberate on everything concerning their "common affairs." It is the idea of man's controlling his conditions of existence through human association. It is an eminently *natural* political idea.

The most striking fact about Europe's history is that neither the city-state nor the empire, nor a combination of the two, provided the form under which Europe reconstituted its political organization. Instead, monarchy was invented.[1]

The third form was the *Church*. To be sure, the Church cannot be placed on the same plane as the empire and the city-state. Organizing men's social and political life is not its raison d'être. But by its very existence and distinctive vocation, it posed an immense political problem to the European peoples. This point must be stressed: the political development of Europe is understandable only as the history of answers to problems posed by the Church, which was a human association of a completely new kind. Each institutional response created in its turn new problems and called for the invention of new responses. The key to European development is what might be called, in scholarly terms, the *theologico-political problem*.

The Church posed two problems to the European peoples, one circumstantial, the other structural. The circumstantial problem is well known: in the general disintegration following the barbarian invasions, the Church had to take on social and political functions not carried out by civil authorities. Thus an "unnatural" amalgam of secular functions and specifically religious ones was formed. The structural problem is also well known, but it is important to formulate it precisely.

The definition that the Church gave itself embodied a contradiction. On the one hand, the good that it provided—salvation—was not of this world. "This world," "Caesar's world," did not interest it. On the other hand, it had been assigned by God himself and by his Son the mission of leading men to salvation, for which the Church, by God's grace, was the unique vehicle. Consequently it had a right or duty to oversee everything that could place this salvation in peril. But since all human actions were faced with the alternative of good and evil (except those actions considered "immaterial"), the Church had a duty to oversee all human actions. And among human actions, the most important were those carried out by rulers. Therefore, in accordance with its raison d'être, the Church had to exercise its vigilance with the keenest attention, seeing to it that rulers did not order the ruled to commit acts that endangered their salvation or allow their subjects the liberty to commit such acts. Thus the Church was led—logically and not circumstantially—to claim the supreme power, the *plenitudo potestatis*. The definition of this *potestas* varied considerably, depending on whether it was conceived of as *directa* or *indirecta,* but the political impact of its claim remained essentially the same. This claim reached its full extent with the Gregorian reform at the end of the eleventh century. At that time the *ecclesia christiana* was considered the only true *respublica.*

The remarkable contradiction embedded in the Catholic Church's doctrine can be summarized in this way: although the Church leaves men free to organize themselves within the temporal sphere as they see fit, it simultaneously tends to impose a theocracy on them. It brings a religious constraint of a previously unheard of scope, and at the same time offers the emancipation of secular life. Unlike Judaism and Islam, the Church does not provide a law that is supposed to govern concretely all of men's actions in the earthly city.

It might be objected that the Church of the Middle Ages always aimed at theocracy and not at the liberation of secular space. There is something to this objection. However, we must consider not only what the Church did directly, but also what it made possible through the contradiction I have indicated. The Church maintained that its control over all political regimes—monarchies, city-states, or empires—was exercised indifferently. By this very fact, it acknowledged that it did not wish to impose a particular political regime. Consequently, when the secular world later regained its strength, it had the latitude to seek the political form that could best resist the Church's claims. In other words, the struggle against the Church's theocratic side was made possible and in a sense authorized by the side that declared Caesar's domain to be free.

On what political bases, then, did the secular world tend to organize itself in order to confront the Church's claims? Let us examine the resources of the two available political forms we have mentioned.

First, the city-state. Up to the sixteenth century, city-states were prevalent in certain regions of Europe (Northern Italy, Flanders, Northern Germany). The historical reasons for this do not concern us here. What is striking is that this political form was overcome by a kind of incapacity to expand or even to endure. This fact stems, of course, from the instability specific to this form of political organization. Civil strife between factions often led to the paralysis and even self-destruction of the city-state, as the chronicles of the Greek and Italian city-states eloquently attest. To these natural reasons were added reasons related to the presence and influence of the Church. On this point two apparently contradictory remarks must be made. On the one hand, when facing the Church, the city-states were relatively weak; they found it difficult to stand up to it. On the other, they were very unfriendly to the Church, which returned the compliment.

City-states were ideologically weak: they were "particulars" facing two "universals," the Empire and the Church. Each faction within the European city-state tended to rely on the support of one of these universals (Guelphs and Ghibellines in Florence) or to rely also on some foreign monarchy. Furthermore, the city-states had an extremely intense, indeed tumultuous, political life. The interests and passions of its citizens were naturally turned toward worldly matters. The city-state thus tended to constitute an especially closed world, one especially resistant to the Church's influence. Finally, the natural position of its citizens was to assert their independence. On these three points, monarchy presented altogether different characteristics.

Too inimical structurally to the Church's claims, the city-state was at the same time too weak to set up a political form capable of successfully asserting itself against the Church while acceding to certain of its demands. Florence is a good example. Perhaps it will be objected that an atypical situation prevailed in Italy, since there the pope was a temporal prince. In reality, even in Italy, the Church's strength was essentially spiritual. The pope was never actually able to carry on a war alone; at the time of the papacy's greatest prestige, he was unable to command adequate obedience even in Rome. Indeed, before the Reformation, he had more influence in England or Germany than in Italy.

In any case, this situation of the Italian city-states had major consequences for all of European history. The mixture of structural hostility and intrinsic weakness in the city-state's relationship with the Church explains to a large extent why Italian city-states developed, and with such aggressiveness, the first truly secular civilization in the Christian world. The great literary assertions of the solidity, independence, and nobility of the secular world were born in Italy: those of Dante, Marsilius of Padua, Boccaccio. This Florentine tradition was then taken up, radically transformed, and made operational for the offensive against the Church launched by that great enemy of Christianity, Machiavelli.

As for the Empire, its actual performance (as distinguished from the prestige of its idea), was in a sense even more modest than that of the city-state. It was not for lack of geniuses: it suffices to mention Charlemagne or Frederick II. Besides, the intrinsic difficulty of the imperial venture in an area as geographically, ethnically, and politically divided as Europe has to be taken into account. Moreover, the place of the empire—the universal—was already occupied, preempted in a way, by the Church. Of course, the Eastern Empire in Constantinople did coexist in a potentially organic union with Christianity. But this union was realized in Constantinople, far from the radiating center of the Christian presence, the pope. Joseph de Maistre, who is particularly reliable on this subject, maintains that if the seat of the Empire was transferred to Constantinople, it was an instinctively opportune impulse: Constantine sensed that "the emperor and the pontiff could not be contained within the same enclosure." He therefore ceded Rome to the pope.[2]

The great political problem in Europe was therefore the following: the nonreligious, secular, lay world had to be organized under a form that was neither city-state nor empire, a form less "particular" than the city-state and less "universal" than the empire, or whose universality would be different from that of the empire. We know that this political form was absolute or national monarchy. Before trying to describe the spiritual and political changes that made its constitution possible, I should like to say briefly why it was structurally superior to the city-state and the Empire when confronting the problem posed by the Church's claims.

Like the emperor, and unlike the city-state, the king was able to lay claim to "divine right" in accordance with the Pauline axiom: "All power comes from God." (The city-states did not because their magistrates, being a plurality, did not fill the first condition for being the image or lieutenant of God: unicity.)[3] Yet in contrast with the emperor, the king did not in principle lay claim to universal monarchy, which limited the extent of the conflict with the Church's universality. Moreover, political life in a kingdom was much more modest than in a city-state, leaving men freer to dedicate themselves to matters of the other world. Finally, the natural position of a monarch's subjects was one of obedience, which suited the Church better. Because of these three features, monarchy was much more compatible with the Church than was the city-state. Simultaneously, and paradoxically, with the assertion of divine right the secular king was in principle radically independent from the Church: the king depended directly on God. The practical consequence was that kings tended to place themselves at the head of even the religious organizations of their kingdoms.

The historical fortune of monarchy in the Christian world stems in large part from the fact that this political form permitted a broad acceptance of the Church's presence and, at the same time, possessed an extremely powerful force (the monarch by divine right) for guaranteeing the political body's independence from the Church.

Thus European monarchy had two sides. The first, a "static" one, can be described as the union of throne and altar. The king was a good Christian and submissive son of the Church, and the Church recognized him as king by God's grace and preached obedience to his power. The second was "dynamic": the king tended naturally to assert the political body's total independence from the Church and hence to claim even the religious sovereignty of his kingdom (for example, the nomination of bishops, control of religious orders, and even, in extreme cases such as England, participation in the definition of Christianity's dogmatic content). Whereas in the Middle Ages political bodies were enveloped or incorporated by the Church, every monarchy heading toward absolutism tended to incorporate the Church within its borders. The kingdom became the supreme political body, the human association par excellence. Once this supremacy was permanently established, the kingdom became the "nation," and its "representatives" imposed on the clergy the "civil constitution," establishing the Church's complete subordination to the body politic.

Thus monarchy appeared to be less a regime than a *process*. This explains why the great historical theories formulated in the nineteenth century readily took away its specificity, making it into a simple instrument destined to be thrown on the scrap heap once it accomplished what "history" expected from it. For Marxism, it was the instrument for passing from "feudalism" to "capitalism"; for Guizot, the instrument of "national" unification and "civilization"; for Tocqueville, it made possible the passage from "aristocracy" to "democracy."[4] These interpretations are of unequal worth, but they all attempted to give an intelligible content to the intuition that monarchy had set "history" in motion, the modern history of Europe, a directed, meaningful, "irresistible" history. Monarchy broke the natural rhythm of political history in Europe, and only in Europe.

The natural rhythm of a body politic can be roughly described as follows. In foreign policy, it fosters territorial expansion up to the point that this expansion threatens its defeat. In domestic policy it involves either conservatism, leading to the petrification of the regime, or a displacement traditionally described as "cyclical" among political forms, predetermined and constant in their essential characteristics: aristocracy, democracy, anarchy, despotism, monarchy. But European monarchy instead set in motion a political evolution leading to the incessant (and not at all cyclical) transformation of the internal constitution of states, one perpetually producing new political and social forms. Monarchy set history in motion, and we are still living with the consequences.

What explains the extreme originality and unequalled dynamism of European monarchy? It was the stable compromise between the religious sacred and the civic sacred, making the king the keystone of the sacred system. But in spite of all his ostentatious religious attributes, in spite of the coronation rites, sacred rituals, and occasional miracles, the king in Europe was never able to play the role that emperors played in the East. There, although the emperor might launch himself into the most extravagant conquests, he remained the great preserver of his society and its civilization. This passively sublime, or sublimely passive role, was forbidden the king in the West: there he had to *act* continuously, and act on *his* society.

What was the principle of this action? The king could not seize and retain the things most sacred to Christianity. (The figure of the king as Christ, for example, did not succeed in acquiring a lasting consistency, for obvious reasons.)[5] Instead he naturally took on the task of forming the political body as one whole, essentially distinct from the Church. He undertook the establishment of the secular city, the *civitas hominum;* he made it one as he himself was one. In principle, of course, the Church left man free to organize the earthly city as he saw fit. But the king alone was capable of taking on the responsibility and effectively assuming this role left to man.

I have just tried to give a very schematic definition of the original problem of European political history. Only by looking at it does the subsequent political development become intelligible. One can present this problem in an almost mathematical form: "given the characteristics of the Catholic Church, find the political form X that makes it possible to ensure the secular world's independence." Since the city-state and the Empire are ruled out, that leaves monarchy. There is much less artifice than one might think in such a presentation, even if it benefits from the advantages of retrospection: this particular problem was certainly, over many centuries, the major problem faced by European peoples. In formulating it in this way, I am presupposing no particular interpretation of Christianity's meaning, or even of man's political condition. Moreover, by placing ourselves in the perspective of the actors themselves, we unlearn what we know (or think we know) about our history. We give ourselves a chance of avoiding subsequent recourse to concepts born after the Church's political defeat in the great battles that concern us, especially that of secularization. We can now understand the notions that made it possible to envisage and implement modern politics, the notions thanks to which we consider ourselves modern. They were born in and arise from this polemical situation. Now we must try to grasp more precisely the spirit in which they were first elaborated.

CHAPTER II

Machiavelli and the Fecundity of Evil

I cannot here describe them all in full;

My ample theme impels me onward so:

What's told is often less than the event.

—*Inferno*, 4.145–47

IN THE BEGINNING, Europe was dominated by the idea of Christian salvation. It was not easy to escape the Church's hold, since it was supported not only by the external power of a dominating institution, but also and especially, by a spiritual conviction. People might very well have wanted to revolt against this great power authorized by Christ. But how could they have conceived what they vaguely desired? How could they have conceived of the secular rights of "nature" that they wanted to set against the Church? It seems obvious to us today because the undertaking triumphed. But in the thirteenth or fifteenth century things were not so clear.

The first major attempt to emancipate man's political nature took place around 1300 in Italy. It was at this time that the rediscovery of Aristotle's works, thanks to their translation into Latin, had its full effect. This great intellectual event was also a great political event. Up to that time, ancient thought had hardly been known in Western Christendom except for the fragments preserved by the Church Fathers, Saint Augustine in particular. Whether approved or criticized, ancient thought had been used for Christian ends. By the fourteenth century it could speak for itself, in its own words, or at least in remarkably faithful translations. That meant that the natural, or secular, world found itself potentially emancipated from Christian categories, and in control of its own destiny. The Church's exclusive intellectual reign was over. It was at this time, in Italy, that opposition to the papacy's political power found its first classic expressions, in the works of Dante and Marsilius of Padua.[1] It was in this place and at this time that European thought fell into step with the political situation.

This first effort was short-lived. The subsequent development of European politics did not follow the principles proposed by Dante or Marsilius. There was certainly a contextual reason for this: Dante and Marsilius placed their political hopes in a regeneration of the Empire. We have seen that this solution was not viable. But there was also a fundamental intellectual reason for their failure: their Aristotelianism, thanks to which they could assert the consistency, richness, and nobility of the natural world, did not allow them to guarantee the independence of politics from the Church's claims. Why was this? Why did the secular world's emancipation from the Church not follow the principles of rediscovered classical antiquity? Why was political modernity not simply a prolonged and expanded Renaissance? Why did it later break with Aristotle and Cicero, its first allies, as well as with the Church?

The principles of classical antiquity were not sufficient for gaining the secular world's independence from the Church. Aristotle interpreted human life in terms of *goods* and *ends,* all organized in a *hierarchy.* Thus his teaching made it possible for Dante and Marsilius to describe with great subtlety the structure of secular life, to show its goodness and dignity. But by presenting human life as a hierarchy of goods and ends, Aristotle's teaching was vulnerable to the Christian claim that the good brought by the Church is greater, the end it reveals is higher, than any merely natural good or end. Consequently, Aristotle's philosophy could be used *both* to express the Church's claim to earthly sovereignty *and* to express the world's protest against the Church. This is why the greatest Aristotelian after Aristotle was a doctor and saint of the Church: Thomas Aquinas. Thomas believed that Aristotle's philosophy contained everything accessible to natural reason. The Christian revelation added other, higher truths to these natural ones, but without invalidating them: "Grace perfects nature, it does not destroy it."[2]

Aristotle's philosophy could thus be used in two conflicting ways: to oppose the Church or to strengthen the Church. The fact that it lent itself to both of these uses sufficed for demonstrating that it could not be the basis for a new political definition of relationships between the secular city-state and the Church. It was too heavy a weapon, which fell naturally from the hands of the one using it into those of his adversary. In the end, the Church knew best how to hold on to it, and it consecrated Thomas as its *Doctor communis,* "universal teacher." But the Thomist doctrine did not give an answer to the politically most urgent question. If I assume that nature has its own goodness and that grace has a superior but not conflicting one, if I assume that man has two unequal but equally legitimate ends, which one must I obey here and now? The Church, taught by Thomas, replied: one must consult prudence, heightened by faith. This answer could not satisfy those who wanted to define the independence of the natural world in a clear-cut and incontestable way. Aristotle, whether interpreted by Thomas, Dante, or Marsilius, did not enable them to solve our theologico-political problem.

The problem was finally resolved, or at least the case decided, two centuries later by Machiavelli. As noted above, it was in Dante's and Marsilius's time that European political thought fell into step with the political situation. It might be added that with Machiavelli political thought became a full participant in the political situation. Henceforth, it was impossible to understand political history without having previously grasped the broad outlines of the history of political thought.

Those, like Dante and Marsilius, who considered Aristotle's thought to be universally valid still had to admit that it had been born in a radically different political context. The Greek city-state, unlike the Italian city-state, had no experience with the political claims of a universal Church. Thus they had to assert the universal validity of his thought and yet subject it to considerable modifications. We have noted the most important of these modifications: Marsilius and Dante argued in favor of the Empire, a political form regarded by Aristotle as inferior to the city-state, even barbarous. With Machiavelli, it was the *modern experience*—he speaks of his *lunga esperienza delle cose moderne* in his Dedicatory Letter to *The Prince* (written in 1513)—that found its own expression. In Machiavelli modernity found an interpretation of itself that determined the orientation of the European mind, and hence of European political history, from that moment on.

But is it not wildly arbitrary to attribute such power to one man? Only a complete account of the development of modern thought and politics after Machiavelli could justify crediting him with a founding role. But in any case we are not ascribing "superhuman" power to the man. The interpretation of modern experience through Machiavelli simply sheds a particularly brilliant light on certain of its fundamental aspects. For it was in the service of a political project, the radical discrediting of the Church's political claims, that numerous men who nurtured this project used Machiavelli to guide their thought and action. By basing themselves on his thought, they transformed the political world: from simple interpretation, from a "theoretical" point of view, it became a part of "real" life. It compelled recognition even from those who had not shared the original project.

I am not about to analyze Machiavelli's thought in detail: first because it is not a part of the principal theme of this essay, next because it is especially subtle, and thus especially resistant to a succinct presentation. I shall confine myself essentially to the idea that everyone, even those who have not read him, has of Machiavelli—that is, to the surface of his work, because it is this surface that influenced men's minds. With an author of Machiavelli's rank, the surface contains, so to speak, the depth.[3]

Machiavelli was Florentine. His "experience of modern things" was the experience of political life in a city-state. We have seen that the city-state was both particularly unfriendly toward the Church and particularly vulnerable when dealing with it. This situation of a quite powerless hostility naturally led to the idea of radically excluding religion from the city-state, of closing off completely the city-state from religion's influence. Certain historians consider that Machiavelli and those who followed him were not hostile to religion as such, only to its excesses and corruptions. But the only way to protect oneself permanently from these excesses and corruptions was to exclude all influence—"good" or "bad"—of religion on civic life.

What do we know about Machiavelli when we know nothing about him? We know that he taught *evil:* how to take and keep power by ruse and force, how to carry through a conspiracy to a successful conclusion. He taught that one must not threaten or insult one's enemy, but that when one has the chance to kill him, then it must be done. We moderns, who like abstract words, readily speak of Machiavelli's political "realism." And it is true that in political "reality" there are murders, conspiracies, coups d'état. But there are also periods and regimes without murders, or conspiracies, or coups d'état. The absence, so to speak, of these wicked actions is also a "reality." Thus, speaking of Machiavelli's "realism" means having accepted his point of view: "evil" is politically more significant, more substantial, more "real" than "good."

That there have been many evils, many violent, wicked, and cruel actions in political life was not taught to men by Machiavelli. They have always known it: how can the obvious be ignored? It is true, however, that the most authoritative authors dealing with political matters did not emphasize this point. Above all they saw in politics the goods that it brought. For Aristotle, looking properly at the city-state meant considering it according to its end: the city-state was the only framework within which man could fulfill his nature as a rational animal, by practicing the civic end moral virtues that permitted him to demonstrate his excellence. Aristotle knew very well that political life has its pathology, its revolutions, its changes of regimes, often accompanied by violence; he devoted book 5 of his *Politics* to them. But to have concentrated men's attention exclusively on these phenomena would have caused them to lose sight of their own end and that of the city-state.

Machiavelli on the contrary persuades us to fix our attention exclusively, or almost exclusively, on pathologies. He wants to force us to lose what, after having read him, we shall be tempted to call our "innocence." Machiavelli is the first of the "masters of suspicion." Not long ago this term was applied to Marx, Nietzsche, and Freud. The characterization is justified inasmuch as these three authors urged us to doubt our best motives. But Machiavelli was the first to carry suspicion to the strategic point of men's life: their political life. His suspicion has never left us since. Just listen to this portrait of the soul suffering from suspicion:

> And it is not just in affairs of the heart that this moral weakening, this powerlessness of lasting impressions can be noticed: it is happening everywhere. Fidelity in love is a force like religious belief, like the enthusiasm for liberty. Now we have no force left. We no longer know how to love, or to believe or to desire. Everybody doubts the truth of what he says, smiles at the vehemence of what he asserts, and hastens the end of what he is feeling.[4]

One of the most deeply rooted traits of the modern soul is doubt of the good, the smile of superiority and mockery, the passion for losing one's innocence. To understand how modern politics was set in motion and developed, one must have previously grasped the change in what has to be called *the status of the good*.

How did Machiavelli go about trying to convince us of the central character of evil in politics? What he liked to study best were "extreme situations": foundings of city-states, changes in regimes, conspiracies. In contrast with Aristotle, he described political life from the perspective of its beginnings or origins—often violent and unjust—and no longer from the perspective of its end. He did not deny that in ordinary circumstances civic life can be quite peaceful, that what men call justice can reign there to an appreciable degree. He simply suggested that this "ordinary" morality depends on—or is influenced by—an "extraordinary" morality. The "good" happens and is maintained only through the "bad." Machiavelli did not erase the distinction between good and evil. On the contrary, he preserved it—and he had to, if he wanted to establish the scandalous proposition that "good" is founded by "evil."

It is easy to grasp the consequences of this point of view on the definition of the city-state and its relationship to religion. It considers the city-state an artificial island constructed by violent means. It is not open to anything beyond itself; it is intelligible only in relation to what brings it about. That means that it becomes unwise and even absurd to want to "improve" or "perfect" the city-state's "good" thanks to a "superior" one that religion would undertake to provide. Such a contribution would only disturb the natural functioning of the city-state. An example will suffice. Christianity produced a certain softening of mores. The political consequence of this was that generally, when a city-state was captured, men were no longer run through with a sword and the women and children were no longer reduced to slavery. Machiavelli shows that from the moment that the citizen's identification of his instinct for self-preservation with the instinct for the city-state's preservation is lost, the motivating force of civic life and morality is fatally weakened. The public good can only be brought about by the power of violence and fear. To insist on the violent conditioning of the city-state, or to point out the political evils produced by Christianity's intrusion into civic life, therefore amounts to the same thing: the political order is now a closed circle having its own foundation within itself, or rather below itself. To assert the necessity and fecundity of evil is now to assert the self-sufficiency of the earthly, secular order.

Up to this point, I have limited myself to recalling the flavor of Machiavelli's teaching, more than the teaching itself. Let me risk a brief incursion into the substance of his argument, in chapter 9 of *The Prince*. There we learn that the city-state has a fundamental division, that between the *common people* and the *nobility*. These two groups are compared with two "diverse humors" of the body politic: the common people do not want to be oppressed, the nobles want to oppress them. One sees that neither of these two groups has an end that is both positive and good, neither is aiming for a good. The nobles have a positive end, but it is wicked: to oppress. The people have no positive end, only a negative one: not to be oppressed. The "humors" of the city-state do not point toward a positive good for the city-state. According to Machiavelli, only the prince who knows how to gain the support of the people in opposing the nobility, without confusing his interest with that of the people, has the chance to found a stable order.[5]

Let us compare chapter 9 of *The Prince* with book 3 of Aristotle's *Politics*. The themes are the same. This book of the *Politics* is a kind of dialogue between the people and the nobility, between the democrat and the oligarch. It is not Aristotle's teaching that interests us here, but his approach. He shows that both the democrat and the oligarch have good arguments for asserting their respective claims to govern, and that in a tolerably well-organized city-state both claims have to be granted. He also shows that, even when joined or adjusted to each other, these two claims do not bring about justice. To the considerations of freedom, equality, and wealth, one must add that of virtue. In other words, he shows how each claim of the social body, however biased it may be, points toward justice or the good which is both part of the body politic and its end. In Machiavelli's description, each element of the city-state is turned into a "humor"; in Aristotle's, each "humor" is anchored in the good.

Certainly, there is an element of the Machiavellian city-state whose humor can, in a sense, be called good: the common people. The people's desire, after all, is innocent: they do not want to be oppressed. Machiavelli even praises their "honesty," at least relatively speaking. The desire of the people is more honest (*è piu onesto*) than that of the nobility, he says. But it is a completely passive or negative goodness. In Machiavelli's city-state, the good is found only in the mutilated form of the people's innocence. Radically depreciating the pretensions to "virtue" of the nobility, and simultaneously making the people "honest," Machiavelli becomes the first *democratic* thinker.

It is easy now to see the link between the insistence on evil in politics and the assertion of the goodness or honesty of the people. If political action is not organized in view of a good—or, more generally, if no human action has an intrinsically good end—then all the goodness of the world belongs to the innocent passivity of those who ordinarily do not act in political terms, to the people. Leo Strauss remarked that the Machiavellian viewpoint heralded Rousseau's distinction between *virtue* (always painful, most often hypocritical or doubtful) and *goodness* (the innocent passivity of self-love with its headquarters, so to speak, in the people). In this aspect of the Machiavellian analysis, we see a new spiritual mechanism that is going to act powerfully on the development of modern politics and, more generally, of modern sensibility: the discrediting of the idea of the good, coinciding with the elevation of the idea of the people.

Something further should be said about Machiavelli's approach to politics. Aristotle, we have noted, begins by adopting the citizen's point of view. He takes seriously each of the principal claims that spring up in the body politic, accepting them as valid, up to a certain point. Citizens consider their claims as the whole of justice; Aristotle corrects their excess by showing that such claims are only a part of justice. At the same time, Aristotle stands outside the city-state. He puts the accent on the rights of virtue, which tend to be ignored in a political life divided between the people and the nobles, democrats and oligarchs. Nonetheless, his position of exteriority and superiority is based on a certain form of community between the philosopher and the city-state. The good aimed for by the city-state, and which it can attain in the most favorable circumstances, points toward a superior and ultimate good that can be grasped only by the philosopher through contemplation. In a word, it is the idea of the good that permits the philosopher to be superior to the city-state, to understand it better than it understands itself, yet also to understand it from within as it understands itself.

With Machiavelli, this medium of communication between the philosopher and the city-state, the good, disappears. The philosopher is completely exterior to the city-state, understanding it better than it understands itself and exposing its "actual truth."[6] But the nobles would not recognize their motives and aspirations in the unique desire to oppress; the people would see in their claims a more positive end than the mere absence of oppression. So, can one say that Machiavelli really understands the aspirations of the citizens better than they themselves do? If nothing connects the city-state's "humors" to the philosopher's search for truth, who will support the "actual truth" when it is found? In a world where nothing can be called intrinsically good, will the knowledge of this truth be an exception? It is not certain that Machiavelli offers us the means to answer these questions. Machiavelli's city-state is a closed totality that he understands completely because he remains completely exterior to it.

This position occupied by Machiavelli is radically new in the history of philosophy and politics. To understand the meaning of life in the city-state, philosophers like Plato and Aristotle took seriously the citizens' viewpoint by adopting it, even if it subsequently meant pointing out its limits and transcending it. Other philosophers deliberately placed themselves outside civic life, with little concern about understanding the citizens' point of view even temporarily. Such philosophers disdained politics because they thought they had a higher good to contemplate: the order of all the cosmos, the divine, or nature. Machiavelli adopts the paradoxical position of keeping himself outside the city-state, while concentrating his attention exclusively on it. He stays on the outside, not to achieve a superior good, but only in hopes of observing it better.

The original, paradoxical character of such a position no longer strikes us today. On the contrary, we recognize in it the requisites of the scientific attitude. We even believe we have understood Machiavelli's originality by noting that he was the first to adopt the "scientific" viewpoint for studying politics. This appraisal, however, often formulated by modern historians, is most likely to blind us both to the nature of political science and to Machiavelli's originality. I have already briefly noted why his "realism" is subject to caution. We can add that to describe political life without taking seriously the citizens' viewpoint is more likely a source of arbitrariness than a guarantee of scientificity. Besides, the development of modern science—strictly speaking, the science of "nature"—is appreciably later than Machiavelli's time. To accept that the modern scientific point of view was first born in his political thought would be to weigh down science itself with political suspicions, instead of covering Machiavelli's politics with the protective coating of science.

An incomparably more plausible and pertinent explanation of Machiavelli's originality is available. After all, in Machiavelli's time, there was another viewpoint claiming to be radically exterior and superior to politics, while pretending, from this position, to act within the city-state: the religious viewpoint of the Church. This position from which one can see politics from the exterior, as subject to intervention, did not have to be invented by Machiavelli; it was furnished to him by his enemy, the Church. Adopting it was not an epistemological exploit, it was, in military language more congruous with Machiavelli's, to fight the enemy on his own ground.

Of course, the Church's position of exteriority was based on a specific raison d'être, something really different from political life: the worship of God, spiritual perfection. It was based on the supposed superiority of the religious good to the political good. Machiavelli's entire approach consists of occupying this position so as to attack the very foundations of the Church's autonomy and of its right to intervene in the city-state. By interpreting the body politic as a closed totality founded on violence, Machiavelli established that the "good" brought by the Church tended to destroy rather than perfect the city-state, that the idea of the good had no support in the nature of human things.

One of Machiavelli's texts, perhaps the most famous, confirms this thesis. In chapter 6 of *The Prince* he compares "armed prophets" to "unarmed ones" and concludes that "all the armed prophets conquered and the unarmed ones were ruined." There is, however, one "unarmed prophet" who could be considered, especially by Machiavelli, as a "conqueror": Jesus Christ. And what is Machiavelli himself, who writes tempting books instead of committing terrible deeds, if not an "unarmed prophet"? Machiavelli is, in his own eyes, that unarmed prophet who is trying to disarm the teaching of the greatest of the unarmed prophets. In this respect, Machiavelli is more an antireligious religious reformer than a philosopher. He tried to change the maxims that actually govern men's lives.

Machiavelli did not elaborate the idea of an institution capable of opposing the encroachments of the Roman Church. That was accomplished by Hobbes. Instead, by discrediting the idea of the good, Machiavelli persuaded men to consider evil—whether ruse, force, violence, or "necessity"—as the principal source of the political order.

To conclude, let us read a brilliant passage from chapter 7 of *The Prince:*

> Once the duke [Cesare Borgia] had taken over Romagna, he found it had been commanded by impotent lords, who had been readier to despoil their subjects than to correct them, and had given their subjects matter for disunion, not for union. Since that province was quite full of robberies, quarrels, and every other kind of insolence, he judged it necessary to give it good government, if he wanted to reduce it to peace and obedience to a kingly arm. So he put there Messer Remirro de Orco, a cruel and ready man, to whom he gave the fullest power. In a short time Remirro reduced it to peace and unity, with the very greatest reputation for himself. Then the duke judged that such excessive authority was not necessary, because he feared that it might become hateful; and he set up a civil court in the middle of the province, with a most excellent president, where each city had its advocate. And because he knew that past rigors had generated some hatred for Remirro, to purge the spirits of that people and to gain them entirely to himself, he wished to show that if any cruelty had been committed, this had not come from him but from the harsh

nature of his minister. And having seized this opportunity, he had him placed one morning in the piazza at Cesena in two pieces, with a piece of wood and a bloody knife beside him. The ferocity of this spectacle left the people at once satisfied and stupefied.

This text is a marvelous illustration of how the civil and political order is enveloped and supported by violence. In this episode, Machiavelli distinguishes three types of violence: the diffuse violence of the impotent lords (violent anarchy); the repressive violence of Remirro de Orco (reestablishing order); and the violence exercised against Remirro de Orco. The second type of violence reestablishes order but leaves the citizens prey to resentment because of the cruel acts committed. The third type purges them of their resentment: the citizens or subjects are *satisfatti e stupidi.* These men are *satisfied,* they are not happy. They do not participate in a good, they are delivered from an evil. They are delivered from a first evil, violence and fear, by another evil, cruel repression; from a second evil, resentment, they are healed by a third evil, fear. This "homeopathic" approach purges them of hate by letting survive just the right amount of fear; and fear is always needed. The political order becomes the alchemy of evil, the suppression of fear through fear.

Thomas Hobbes will see the very logic of the human order in the series of actions and feelings dramatically described by Machiavelli. The absolute monarchy, the "Leviathan" described by Hobbes, is the institutionalization of Cesare Borgia's actions at Cesena.

CHAPTER III

Hobbes and the New Political Art

Iт ıs noт possıble to deduce from Machiavelli the legitimacy, suitability, or even the need for particular institutions. It can be asked if, in his world of actions that judiciously cause fear, there is even a place for institutions. Every institution implies a positive goodness of the body politic, which seems alien to Machiavelli's vision. There is, however, one element of his city-state that has something of this "goodness": the people, who do not want to be oppressed. In themselves they do not have the means of founding a new political order; but if one wants to construct a positive institution, while remaining faithful to Machiavelli's principles, it is on this side that one has to look. With Hobbes, in fact, it is the people themselves—not as part of the body politic distinct from the elite, but as all those wishing to live free from fear—who are going to take the political initiative. The basic needs of all individuals—security, peace—are going to be the foundations of the legitimate political institution. The men whom Borgia's exploits leave *satisfatti e stupidi* are going to want to be satisfied, and they are going to know how this satisfaction can be obtained. To be satisfied, they are going to become intelligent.

It is impossible to go further without giving at least a summary idea of the context and circumstances of Hobbes's work. It was born in an emergency: Hobbes saw the preparation for and outbreak of the English Civil War, which culminated in the execution of King Charles I in 1649. This war, inseparably political and religious, was the most dramatic expression of the theologico-political problem in its postmedieval form. It raged for several years and raised related questions: What is the king's function, what is the meaning of the monarchical institution, and what is religion's place in the body politic?

Henry VIII had severed the English monarchy from Rome at the time of the Lutheran Reformation. But Henry VIII was not Protestant: he persecuted impartially both Protestants and Catholics. It was a purely political secession: the English body politic through its monarch declared itself independent from Rome. Being independent from Roman religion did not mean being emancipated from religion, only that the king or queen became the head of the kingdom's religion. But the head of what religion? The monarch who escaped the tutelage of Roman priests and theologians had to make himself a theologian, if not a priest. It was under Elizabeth, after the Catholic reaction of Mary Tudor, that the Protestant character of the English monarchy was fixed and England's religious destiny was sealed.

The right to determine his subjects' religion that the king assumed placed him in a singularly exposed situation. By choosing Protestantism, or a version of it, as the state religion, he consecrated the authority of this interpretation of Christianity. He thus gave weapons to the followers of its most vigorous or radical version, the Puritans, who contested the state religion and the state itself. At the same time, whatever his desire might possibly have been, the monarch could not go back to Catholicism, thereafter considered as a foreign and hostile religion. Thus, the fruitless efforts of Elizabeth's successors to impose a Christianity of royal definition which could satisfy neither all the Protestants nor, of course, those who had remained Catholic. The king became, as far as religion was concerned, a foreigner to his people.

During his perilous effort to remove his people from Roman tutelage, the king was forced to rely on their "representatives." Whether this support was given voluntarily or had to be extorted, the result was the same: the House of Commons, whose original role was that of representing the English before the king, saw its own legitimacy consolidated, its "national" legitimacy crystallized. The religious discord provided the representatives with the occasion, the temptation, and the means of defining the body politic independently of the king. Simultaneously, the definition of the body politic having come to depend on a religious opinion which, it had been learned, was not fixed, the emancipation from royal authority naturally led to the decomposition of this body into groups corresponding to diverse religious opinions. These groups readily became enemies. That being the case, Hobbes saw clearly that the only way of saving royal authority, and thus civil peace, was to detach completely the king's power from religion by making the king fully sovereign over it.

What, according to Hobbes, are the causes of the English Civil War? He distinguishes two, one secular, the other religious. The secular cause is found in the influence of the universities, which educate the elite; the religious cause is found in the influence of the Presbyterians, or Puritans, who are by and large made up of the people. The universities' influence stems from classical studies, from Greek and Roman models glorifying "freedom." The Puritan influence stems from a religious conception attributing to everyone who shares it the right and duty to obey individual "inspiration," and the right and duty to "dogmatize." These two influences conspire to foment the spirit of disobedience.

Thus at the origin of Hobbes's construction lay the two great doctrines of protest against the Church's political power: classical republicanism

(Aristotle and Cicero) and Protestantism. These led to a political and social catastrophe. Now, notice that these two great movements consisted of appealing to a prestigious past (antiquity) or a pure one (primitive Christianity) against a corrupted present. Or, put differently, the Catholic confusion between nature and grace, expressed in Aristotelian scholasticism, naturally led to appeals to pure nature (antiquity) or to grace alone (Protestantism). Why did these two appeals lead to an unprecedented disorder?

The problem was that, whatever the intrinsic merits of classical antiquity and primitive Christianity, these two great doctrines existed in England only as *opinions*. They were available to all, providing a ready-made argument or pretext whenever anyone's vanity inclined him to disobedience. What had in ancient times been experience, now became an opinion that proved to be ruinous for civic life. Consequently—and this is the polemical heart of the Hobbesian vision—the deplorable political effects of these opinions refuted their claim to reflect an experience authoritatively.

Take classical republicanism. Its fundamental thesis was that the city-state was natural, and urged men to rule themselves in freedom. But the effect of this idea's prestige on the actual conduct of men in Hobbes's time was only to set them against each other in the name of freedom. The destructive effect of this opinion was stronger than the supposed political nature of men. Thus, "nature" had to be dismissed as model or reference for political organization. The same was true of Protestantism. Its fundamental thesis was that God bestows his grace on anyone who approaches him with a pure and humble heart, and that such a man, with divine help, will want and do only the good. The experience of the Civil War showed that the claim of "having grace," of being "holy," led to insufferable political arrogance, to disdain for and humiliation of one's neighbor. Hence the conclusion Hobbes drew from the crucial experience of the English Civil War was the following: neither nature nor grace can unite men. Then what can? The only possible response was obvious: *art*.

Traditionally, art was defined as the imitation of nature. If nature was no longer to be the reference, what was to be the model for this new art that Hobbes had to elaborate? Every "model" being an "opinion" on "nature," and every opinion being a principle of disorder, it was necessary to develop an art that needed no model. Political art needs a foundation stronger than any opinion. In other words, until this point the basis of political action had been the idea of the good, whether natural or supernatural. This way of conceiving of action in the city-state failed tragically, because men inevitably have incompatible notions of what is good, an incompatibility that is an unending source of conflicts and wars. But if people are unsure about what is good, they are not unsure about what is evil, or at least about certain evils. There is one evil in particular that is considered by every human being, or at least by most, as the greatest evil; and they recognize it not through reasoning, always contestable, but through the grip of a passion that nothing can quell. That evil is death. The foundation, stronger than all opinion, of the new political art will be this passion: *the fear of death.*

This reminds us of Machiavelli and the episode in Cesena. The Florentine and the Englishman both count on fear for constructing the new city-state. But Machiavelli leads us to believe that fear, insofar as it is politically effective and beneficial, is created by the prince endowed with *virtù*: this efficacious fear is an effect of art. In Italy the human association had not been fully destroyed, it was only passive or condemned to a helpless feverishness. A sort of shameful compromise between the city-states and the Church, between nature and grace, preserved a certain consistency in it. It was thus advisable to reactivate it by a judicious use of fear. In Hobbes's England, on the contrary, the power of disassociation of opinion had ruined human association as such. The conflict of opinions over the good had produced the war of all against all, which prevented all social, intellectual, and economic life. Everyone was racked by the fear of death. The incompatibility of opinions regarding the good had produced absolute evil. It was from this point that one had to rise up, to reconstruct a new political organization invulnerable to the conflict of opinions. The plague of fear had to be made into the *cause* of the salutary art. The principle of this new order would not be the good one was seeking, but the evil one was fleeing.

It will be said, however, that civil war is an exceptional circumstance: it is impossible to conceive of the ordinary ends and means of political life by starting from it. Hobbes replies that civil war, the war of all against all, is "the natural condition of mankind." In his eyes, the political and religious strife of his country is only a particularly cruel manifestation of behavior natural to men when they live without recognized and undisputed masters. Even in times of civil peace, that is, in "normal" circumstances, Hobbes observes the permanent presence of fear, distrust, aggressiveness. Do not men lock their doors at night and even, within their houses, lock their chests, thus proving that they are permanently afraid, not only of their fellow citizens but also of their servants and even of their children?[1] Careful observation also reveals that man's life in society is dominated by pride, conceit, and vainglory, the desire to get the upper hand over one's neighbor, to have one's superiority recognized. In a period of civil peace, when the legitimate sovereign is recognized and obeyed, man's pride inflicts and receives only wounds of pride. But let the sovereign be uncertain or contested, let civil war take over, and exacerbated pride will become destructive and murderous, laying into the property and even the lives of rivals. The rivalry of all with all thus becomes what it was implicitly: the war of all

against all. Such is the natural condition of mankind. The Greek idea of a
benevolent nature, constituted by a group of hierarchical goods of which
the city-state would make men participants, is completely ruined.

But, some will say, this criticism of human nature is simply the Christian
criticism of humanity in the grip of original sin. It is true that this picture of
the human condition allies Hobbes with the gloomiest of Christian moral-
ists. It was at this time that Pascal wrote: "All men naturally hate each
other," and also, "Each self is the enemy and would like to tyrannize all the
others." But it is precisely when he appears closest to an essential aspect of
the Christian vision that Hobbes turns it upside down. In this imminent
war of all against all, "the natural condition of mankind," the worst
actions cannot be considered faults or sins. In a situation where the life of
each person is perpetually in danger, all acts are covered by legitimate
defense; even the seemingly least provoked attack can always be considered as preventive. Like Machiavelli's prince in the uncertainty and violence of political existence, each person in the state of nature is sole judge
of the conduct necessary for preserving his life. If such is the natural
condition of mankind, it is all too clear that men's desires and passions
cannot be sins, either in themselves or by nature. If the most atrocious
murders can be justified, it is obvious that notions such as morality, right
and wrong, and sin have no meaning in the state of nature. Good and evil
do not exist by nature. They have meaning only once the state of nature has
been surmounted, once public authorities have promulgated laws that
define these notions.

The Hobbesian description of the state of nature made it possible to
reject simultaneously the claims of the classical view of nature and the
Christian view of grace: the former by showing that nature is not good, or
that life according to nature is the recapitulation of all evils; the latter by
showing that these evils do not have their source in sin, but in necessity,
and therefore require healing by art rather than by grace. Thanks to a new
art, a new definition of the political good is born from this absolute evil.

The necessity that forces men in the state of nature to do what the
ordinary opinion calls evil, also binds them, although less directly, to what
this same opinion calls good. The state of nature is unbearable for man: in
the war of all against all, each person's life is "solitary, poore, nasty, brutish
and short"—especially, short.[2] The threat of violent death hangs over
everything, whereas man wants nothing so much as to shield himself from
death. And this war's most abundant source is precisely each person's
desire to preserve his life. The fear of death pushes men to this murderous
conduct which places them in mortal danger. This situation is absurd, or at
best a logical contradiction. To solve a logical contradiction, it is not
necessary to be good, or generous or courageous, or pious; a little inge-
nuity will do. It suffices to have that quality that modern men are going to

prize above all else: intelligence, the faculty to solve problems. And how could men fail to be intelligent, when they are forced to it by the most imperious passion of all, the fear of death? Human reason, observing the absurdity of this war, is going to seek a means of peace. More precisely, what one calls reason is born from this necessity, which is experienced and recognized through passion: it is the faculty of inventing means or producing effects. The new political art will be the good use of this faculty. What Hobbes clarified is the fact that men, if they want to be satisfied, are constrained to be intelligent.

To reason born from and educated by fear of death, the very terms of this political problem point the way toward its solution. To say that in the state of nature each person can do anything that he deems useful for defending himself, means that each person has a right over everything (a *jus in omnia*), including the bodies of others.³ This unlimited right of each person ensues necessarily from the war of all against all; it is also the source of war. Only by renouncing this right can each person dry up war's source. This renunciation would be absurd if he did not have a reasonable assurance that each of his neighbors and rivals would do the same. Each person must therefore engage in a mutual covenant to renounce this unlimited right. But "covenants without the Sword, are but words," says Hobbes.⁴ The only possible guarantee of the covenant is in the threat of punishment that will constitute a sanction against all violation. Who will inflict this punishment? The one (or ones) whom the parties to the covenant have chosen. Everyone will renounce his right over everything and will transfer it to the one to whom he entrusts sovereignty, on the condition that this sovereign will promulgate the laws necessary for civil peace, and guarantee (by force if necessary) that they are obeyed.

The right of the sovereign, individual or collective, is necessarily unlimited. His sovereignty is absolute because the right transmitted to him by everyone is unlimited. The sovereign inherits the *jus in omnia* that belonged to each individual in the state of nature; or it might be said that he alone keeps this right, held by all in the state of nature and abandoned by all except him. In this way the sovereign, the Leviathan, is constituted. He is that "artificial man" or "mortal God" who will ensure civil peace.

This briefly, is how Hobbes deduces the necessity of absolutism, if men want to live in peace. One remark immediately comes to mind: it is better not to let oneself be overly impressed by this sovereign's "majesty." What is actually the foundation of his absolute sovereignty? The right of the individual. And what is the source of this right? The humble necessity for self-preservation, for escaping death. Men must no longer be guided by goods or by the good, but by the right that is born from the necessity of fleeing evil. In the moral and political language developed by Hobbes, and which is still ours today, the *right* replaces the *good*. The intensity of moral approval that the ancients gave to the good, the moderns, following Hobbes, gave to the right, the right of the individual. This is the language and "value" of liberalism.

What does it mean to transfer one's unlimited natural right to the sovereign? It means recognizing as mine all actions, whatever they may be, taken by the sovereign. I am the *author* of all the actions taken by my sovereign; he is my *representative*. And the unity of the body politic consists of this: all members of the body have the same representative, the sovereign.

After individual rights, there is another founding category of liberal thought: *representation*. What is the origin of the necessity of representation for the constitution of the body politic? In the state of nature, there is no power, or rather the powers of each person are about equal because men are equal. How does Hobbes establish this important point? By using an argument that can be taken as a joke: in the state of nature, the weakest can always kill the strongest. Is this a weak argument? On the contrary, it is an extremely strong one. If the fundamental human experience is that of evil in the state of nature, if what is most natural is that state of nature, then what is most important in human relations is revealed in this situation. And there is no doubt that in this situation the vulnerability of one person can hardly be very different from the vulnerability of every other person. "You may be more beautiful, more intelligent, more courageous than I, so be it, but I can kill you, by force or by ruse: that is what counts between us."

If men are essentially equal, if their equal powers are neutralized, then political power that binds the body politic is not natural. If it is not natural, then it is artificial: it has to be fabricated. But an artifact is made entirely by the artisan. In the "finished product," there is—other than the raw material, in this case human nature—only the intention and determination of the artisan, the artificer.[5] (By this term, which signifies "artisan," Hobbes designates man in his capacity as creator of the body politic.) Political power incorporates and represents the intention and determination of artisans, who are men in the state of nature desiring peace. Absolute power is only the instrument of the powerless. The ostentatious amplifications of power in the Hobbesian doctrine must not mask a radical weakening of its substance. What is substantial is the equality of the powerless.

What we have here is the matrix of the distinction between civil society and the state. Civil society is the locus of equal rights, and the state is the instrument of this civil society that ensures order and peace. At the same time, the paradox of the Hobbesian doctrine—that the state arises from the civil society over which it exercises absolute power—reflects the fundamental difficulty of the distinction, and of the idea of representation inseparable from it. If civil society is what is natural, and if the state is only its instrument, why is the state detached from society in such a definite way? Why does civil society not simply take it over again, bringing an end to this "alienation"? Conversely, if the body politic exists only through the Representative, then the Representative is more than a mere representative; he gives consistency to civil society and is the source of social existence. The distinction between civil society and the state, and their union through the idea of representation, sets off a natural oscillation between two extreme possibilities: the "withering away" of the state on the one hand, the absorption of civil society by the state on the other. It is a distinction that calls out for negation, a negation that can benefit only one of the two terms.[6]

The relationship between individuals and the sovereign can be formulated in another fashion. If men are equal in the state of nature because the weakest can always kill the strongest, there is no reason why one man rather than the other commands. If obedience cannot be based on nature, but if it is necessary for civil peace, it can have its source only in *convention*. It can be legitimate only when founded on the *consent* of the one who obeys. More generally, according to Hobbes, every obligation necessarily has its source in an action taken by the individual who obeys. If, in the state of nature, everyone does as he pleases—that is, what he deems essential for his self-preservation—in the civil state he also does as he pleases by obeying the sovereign. The individual has consented in principle to what the sovereign orders him to do, since he is the Author of his Representative's actions. I have just used the phrase, "does as he pleases by obeying the sovereign." In a sense it explains very well what Hobbes describes: the subject can neither accuse the sovereign nor put him to death, because that would be tantamount to accusing himself or to committing suicide. There is a basic identity between the subject and the sovereign. Still, such an expression is misleading. Hobbes excludes any transfer of will, any representation of one will by another: will belongs to the individual. Certainly, the subject recognizes all the sovereign's *actions* as his own, but that does not at all signify that the subject recognizes his own will in the sovereign's *will*.

The importance of this question for the problem of democracy is not difficult to see. Democracy, whether direct or representative, implies that the action of the body politic has its motivating force in each person's will, or in a will representing each person's will. Hobbes strongly "identifies" "each subject" and the sovereign, but excludes will from this identification or identity. What is *desired* (*willed*) by "each subject" is the existence of absolute sovereignty, or, more precisely, it is the peace for which absolute sovereignty is the necessary instrument. As for the sovereign's wishes, they are his own. In other words, Hobbes decisively prepares the democratic idea, but remains no less decisively short of it.

The democratic idea, to which we are accustomed from childhood, makes Hobbes's conception seem quite absurd. What does it mean to recognize as one's own actions those one has not willed, actions that can be contrary to everything one wants? Hobbes's absolutism shuttles uncomfortably between identity and difference. But we get the feeling that identity must be the stronger of the two and that it will triumph naturally in the democratic idea, according to which the will of the representative aims at fulfilling the people's will. On the other hand, perhaps the difficulties in Hobbes's position suggest difficulties in the democratic idea that we would not otherwise see.

The strength of the Hobbesian position is that it retains the integrity of the individual. The individual wants what he wants, no one else can want it for him. If then the individual and his will are the unique foundation for political legitimacy, it is clear that the political order, which makes a unity from the plurality of individuals, can come to him only from the outside. Every "community of will," whether with other individuals, or between the individual and the sovereign, would encroach on the individual's will, infringe on his integrity. He could no longer be what he alone can be: the source and foundation of political legitimacy. One is tempted to say that Hobbes is absolutist in spite of his individualism. But, on the contrary, Hobbes is absolutist *because* he is so rigorously individualistic.

If we find it hard to admit such an idea, it is because we have only a very faint idea of what it means to take the individual seriously, to make the individual, and the individual alone, the foundation of all political legitimacy. The individual of whom we speak nowadays is always already implicitly "acculturated," "socialized," determined by "roles"; he is domesticated. We no longer have a clear notion of the man who is, according to us, the source of all legitimacy, and whose particularities and demands continue to affect the social, political, and spiritual evolution of our societies. Hobbes makes us aware that, if there must be something like an individual, a being whose will belongs by right only to himself, then this will can find a rule only in another will that has the force and right to impose obedience on him.

An eloquent proof that Hobbes's individualism is certainly at the source of his absolutism is found in Rousseau's approach, so contrary to Hobbes's and yet so akin to it. Rousseau was the one who best understood Hobbes and who criticized him most profoundly. He understood very well that if one starts seriously from the individual, it is supremely difficult, if not impossible, to avoid absolutism. But since Rousseau was trying to avoid absolutism, while himself starting from the individual, he had to proceed to reinterpret not only political legitimacy but also human nature itself. Everybody knows what a prodigious influence this reinterpretation has had on our ideas, feelings, and mores. Since I shall be speaking about

Rousseau in his chronological place, I shall confine myself here to one remark.[7]

Rousseau shares Hobbes's basic conviction: the will is an individual thing, it cannot be represented. On the other hand, he rejects absolutism: the unified order to be established among individual wills must not come from the outside. Therefore each person's will must be identified with the will of the body politic, or the body politic's will with each person's will, without third-party representation. In addition, every action of an individual will on another must be excluded. From these conditions comes the "general will." In other words, since the individual must not obey another individual, or an absolute sovereign, or a representative, he has only himself to obey. To resolve the political problem induced by seeking political unity among radically independent individuals, Rousseau is led to invent a new definition of man and reason. Man is the being who is capable of obeying a law that he has imposed on himself, and reason is the faculty of commanding oneself, that is, autonomy or self-legislation. One is led to say, using Hobbes's terms, that with Rousseau man becomes the "author" and "artificer" or "maker" of his own humanity, and no longer simply of the body politic. This is not the place to examine the meaning and consequences of such a conclusion. The perplexity into which it throws us, a perplexity that was and remains the motivating force of modern philosophy's evolution since Rousseau, suggests that we ought to consider Hobbes's sober absolutism more sympathetically than we commonly do.

But can this absolutism really succeed in realizing its aim of creating a political unity from radically separated and independent individuals? Certainly it is easy to imagine that individuals obey the sovereign because they are satisfied with the peace he guarantees, or because he threatens them with punishments. Certainly we can conceive of individuals who are strangers to each other becoming one because they have a common representative. But is not this unity through a single Representative, on which Hobbes insists, largely abstract? Based exclusively on the covenant, is it not precisely a simple agreement, and therefore unreal?

In fact, individuals can constitute a real unity only if they are similar or homogeneous. The Hobbesian political problem is to hold together atoms that are both foreign and similar to each other. What makes them enemies is what they have in common; and what makes them capable of living together is also what they have in common. What do they share? Their fundamental passion for power, for ever-increasing power, a desire ceasing only with death; men differ only in the degree of intensity of this desire. It is because they are transformed by this desire that they are perpetually in a state of war, latent or declared. Simultaneously, what makes their unity so difficult is also what makes it possible. If individuals are the quanta of power, then in order to unite they must construct above themselves a quantum of power incomparably superior to their own. More precisely, they must construct above themselves the greatest power they can imagine, a power such that one cannot imagine a greater one. This is the definition of an *unlimited* or *absolute* power.

I have said that Hobbes deduced the political institution from the rights of the individual and from them alone. This is not entirely exact: the individual not only has *rights,* he also has a *nature.* Leviathan can guarantee the individual's rights by unifying the body politic because both Leviathan and man are constituted by power: there is basic homogeneity between the state and society. The device of representation is supported by a conception of man's nature that extends beyond the idea of rights. The "artisan" of absolute power is capable of fabricating that power because, in his being, he too is power, or rather desires power. In this sense, the Hobbesian individual remains something of a political animal.

This individual greedy for power is powerless in the state of nature. What then will he sacrifice in order to accomplish something? Not his power, which is nonexistent or ineffective, but his right to do as he pleases. So as to make a certain power from his impotence he constructs an absolute power above himself. The traditional religious interpretation of royal power signified that the king linked himself directly with God, that he was accountable only to Him, that he was his lieutenant or representative, and that consequently he participated in the omnipotence or sovereignty of God. But the case of the Hobbesian absolute power is completely different. It is no longer an almighty being who gives existence and the meaning of existence to absolute power. On the contrary, it is powerless beings who create Leviathan to remedy their weakness. Absolute power is no longer God's representative, but mankind's; its transcendence no longer has its origins in God's strength but in man's weakness.

Leviathan's power is therefore such that men cannot imagine a greater one. Such a definition reminds one of Saint Anselm's definition of God: *ens quo majus cogitari nequit* (a being such that a greater one is inconceivable). From this nominal definition, Anselm concludes that God exists according to the "ontological" argument.[8] What Hobbes's presentation suggests is that this being does indeed exist, that it actually organizes the human world, but that it is fabricated by men. The political institution is the human device permitting men to make effective and efficient this "idea of the greatest power" that in their impotence they are naturally led to imagine. There is no more subtle way of suggesting that the construction of Leviathan reproduces the genesis of the idea of God: in following the construction of the Hobbesian body politic, we are witnessing the elaboration of the idea of God. Hobbes shows us both how the natural situation of men leads them to conceive of the idea of God, and how human art can appropriate the meaning of this idea, revealing its vanity by this very art.

The political art establishes that religion is both "natural" and "false," and why it can be one or the other without contradiction.

Hobbes creates the political order from human impotence; Aristotle created it from human capacities or strength. Unlike Aristotle's city-state, the Hobbesian body politic does not compose and adjust forces (virtue, wealth, freedom); it relieves weaknesses. Leviathan heals, at least in part, the ills of the "natural condition of mankind." Under Leviathan's hand, the subject finds himself like the faithful under the Church whose grace heals the ills of sinful nature. The body politic constructed by powerless men who conceive of an absolute power is not a city-state, limited by the natural order and thus vulnerable to the intervention of religion. Its genesis repeats and makes effective the gesture by which humanity conceives of the divinity and places itself under its protection. The meaning of the Hobbesian state is to be an artificial Providence.[9] Just as the state of nature neutralizes sin by naturalizing it, Leviathan's absolute power neutralizes grace by making it artificial.

By nature, men quarrel rather than love or help each other. This political problem is so difficult, and its solution so simple in Hobbes, that political discussion faces only clear-cut alternatives. Either the body politic exists and citizens live in civil peace, or it does not and citizens tear each other to pieces. Either the sovereign has the power necessary for fulfilling his mandate and then men enjoy the happiness compatible with their condition, or he lacks it and men experience the disorders and misfortunes of civil war. This means that the comparison between the respective merits of different political regimes seems altogether pointless to Hobbes. Admittedly, one can distinguish between democracy, aristocracy, and monarchy. But whether the sovereign is one, several, or everyone, what is important is that that sovereign have the right to demand complete obedience. Whether he is one, several, or everyone, the sovereign conceives of, promulgates, and enforces respect for the laws that seem to him good or expedient. They are laws only because they are the declaration of his will. One is no more free to disobey the laws in Venice or Lucca than in the realm of the Grand Turk. Of course, monarchy has a certain number of technical advantages based on the fact that a natural individual is the soul of the artificial individual that is the body politic. But the inflexible rule is this: that each citizen must consider the regime under which he lives as the best one. Indeed, he does not even attempt to evaluate it, and obeys in all good conscience everything that the sovereign orders him to do.

However, whether a regime is a monarchy, aristocracy, or democracy, its legitimacy—which is also its mode of generation—is essentially democratic. The foundation of every regime is based on each citizen's consent. The sovereign's power does not belong to him by nature or by grace, it is always given by his subjects. By dismissing the old discussions about the

best regime, by being particularly critical of ancient democracies, by scorn-
ing the monarchies in which Europeans lived, Hobbes contributed powerfully to the making of the modern democratic view. For its partisans,
modern democracy is not one political regime among others; it is the *only*
legitimate organization of men's life in common. Precisely because it is
based on consent, its legitimacy—which is its goodness—is beyond any
doubt. To whoever objects or grumbles, one can always answer: what are
you complaining about? This is what you wanted. And even if you voted
against, it is as though you had voted for, since you committed yourself to
abide by the law of the majority.

Because Leviathan is external to individuals, and because they are the
quanta of its power, the sovereign's absolute power is not in contradiction
with his subjects' liberty. Whatever is outside the obedience of the law is
free; where the law is silent, subjects can do whatever seems good to them.
A quantum of power does everything it can do; it cannot cease to be a
power to act. Wherever the sovereign interposes his law, with the threat of
punishment, the subject obeys. But wherever there is no law he acts freely,
since nothing prevents him from doing so. The law promulgated by the
sovereign is only the device that prevents men/atoms from clashing with
each other; it does not immobilize them. It is similar to those hedges that
prevent one from parking on a neighbor's field, but not from walking on
his path. Hobbes can be called the founder of liberalism because he elaborated the liberal interpretation of the law, a pure human device, rigorously
external to everybody. Such a law does not transform or inform the individual atoms whose peaceful coexistence it is limited to guaranteeing.

Hobbes's thought is thus the common matrix of modern democracy and
liberalism. It founds the democratic idea because it develops the notion of
sovereignty established on each subject's consent. It founds the liberal idea
because it develops the notion of the law as device external to individuals.
It is not clear that the democratic idea of sovereignty and the liberal idea of
the law are easily compatible, since in *Leviathan* these two notions only
link up through absolutism. It is because unlimited sovereignty is external
to individuals that it leaves them free space where the law is silent. If one
abolishes absolutism, that is, the exteriority of sovereignty, then the law
becomes, as Rousseau says, "the register of our wills." The law is no longer
the external condition of my free action, it becomes the very principle of
this action: the liberal notion of the law is dead. If, on the contrary, one
wants to abolish absolutism while maintaining the liberal interpretation of
the law, the very idea of unlimited sovereignty has to be renounced. This is
what Montesquieu will do.

Yet the fact remains that our democratic and liberal societies seem to
have overcome this contradiction. Perhaps not entirely, but such a contradiction is not fatal. The democratic idea of sovereignty and the liberal idea

of the law are contradictory only in their positive aspects, not the negative ones. They have a common "negative matrix": they agree that man has no ends inscribed in his nature, and that the element of human action is not the good or goods. The two definitions, democratic and liberal, alternately prevailed; sometimes they emphasized the sovereignty of the collective will, sometimes the legal liberty of individuals. This contradictory compatibility of the two definitions helps to explain why our democratic and liberal regimes are both remarkably stable and subject to perpetual and rapid social change.

In presenting the dominant ideas of the Hobbesian doctrine, I have placed the emphasis on the themes and difficulties that determined the subsequent development of political thought. I have deliberately neglected—and paradoxically so, given the principal idea of this essay— Hobbes's direct criticism of Christianity. I have tried to suggest that the positive logic of the Hobbesian construction is more fundamental than the direct criticism of religion. Hobbes draws the plans for a body politic invulnerable to Christianity since it reproduces its meaning, making it effective. However, so that the explanation is not incomplete, I must say a few words about Hobbes's radical and influential criticism of religion.

The question is the following: what happens to the duty to obey the sovereign when he orders an action contrary to the subject's idea of God's law or will? What happens to the sovereign's sovereignty in face of a religion that orders men to obey God rather than other men? What I have already said contains the response: everything that is human falls within Leviathan's power, and thus religion also. However much religion may have its origins in God, it still addresses itself to men and is preached by men. Without ever contesting the principle that it is better to obey God than men, Hobbes limits its application so much that this principle becomes politically inoffensive, incapable of moving the masses of men. Moreover, and more radically, he reinterprets the meaning of Christian revelation in such a way that obedience to God tends to merge with obedience to the sovereign.

On the first point, Hobbes's argument is simple but devastating. To believe that God spoke to certain men is to believe that these men speak the truth, it is to believe *them*. The necessity of a human intermediary means that to believe in a revealed God is to believe men. Now, experience teaches us that men are readily liars, or more exactly, that the elevated idea they have of their wisdom often leads them to believe themselves inspired by God. Besides, those who believe themselves to be inspired most often attract partisans, who call themselves disciples. Thus those inspired by God hold a power whose extent depends on the number of their partisans. We know that the desire for power is men's dominant, primordial desire. Therefore we should not be surprised if many an individual, through sheer desire for power, proclaims himself inspired by God. Does not Scripture itself—the Old as well as the New Testament—insist on this point, that there are false prophets? Indeed, that for one truly inspired prophet, there are a hundred or four hundred false ones? The lesson of secular experience is just as clear: each time that an individual or a group of individuals claims to be inspired by God, those who listen to them must be skeptical: the probability is that they are impostors. The safest action is to recognize as prophets only those who are judged as such by the sovereign. If men are convinced by Hobbes's arguments, it is not very likely that any prophets, true or false, will have many disciples.

There remains the case of those who, instead of simply following the prophets, believe themselves to be prophets. Whether sincere or liars, they are inaccessible to reason. Thus they ought to be left to the sovereign's judgment; he will decide whether they constitute a danger to civil peace. If he judges them to be dangerous, the sovereign will use public force to ensure that they can do no harm. The operation will be easy because, thanks to Hobbes's warnings, they will have hardly any disciples. The claims of the "prophets" or "saints" who played such a role in the English Civil War will cease to be a major political threat; they will pose only a simple problem of law and order.

One can wonder whether Hobbes's triumph here is not too complete and even somewhat imprudent. If every claim of divine inspiration is as radically suspect, is not the very root of Christianity in danger? Would one not have to suspect the Apostles and Christ himself? Hobbes asserts that he has no stake in the matter, that he is only reminding us of the vigilance recommended by scripture. Therefore, he accepts that there are (or at least were) true prophets, on whose witness the Catholic church and Protestant confessions are founded. Conceding this—and Hobbes had to concede it if he wanted to avoid suffering the fate reserved for false prophets—a new task faced him. He had to show that scripture itself, exactly interpreted, actually professes Hobbes's own political doctrine: that is, that the civil sovereign is absolute also in religious matters. We shall not follow him in his exegesis. Its conclusion is that it is all the same whether ones says "Church" or "body politic composed of Christians": there is no place in the human world for another representative. There is no need for a power other than civil power.

The fundamental question of the Hobbesian doctrine is that of *obedience:* whom does my conscience tell me to obey? The question is fundamental because if the response is uncertain then civil war ensues. And yet this question is new, or at least the intensity with which Hobbes and his successors ask it is. Of course, in a sense, the question of obedience is always posed in real political life. Yet, it did not play a major theoretical role in the Greek formulation of the political problem. For the Greeks, the important questions were: what is the best political regime? Who is best qualified to command, the people, the rich, the wise, or a man of exceptional virtue? These are the questions Aristotle poses in his *Politics*.

It will be said that the two approaches are essentially the same. If I know who must command, I know whom to obey, and conversely. Here the similarities end. According to Aristotle, the one who commands must be the bearer of the most important human good, the most politically significant, the "best" human good. The candidates whose claims are rejected (actually, only corrected and moderated) also draw their inspiration from significant goods, although they are less important. For Aristotle, to answer the question "Who must command?", is to decide on the basis of a hierarchy of goods; but the goods that are not chosen survive and even obtain some portion of power, once the decisive choice has been made. For Hobbes, on the contrary, the one who has the right to demand obedience has all rights, those who do not have this right have none, or rather have only the rights conceded by the former. Gradation is replaced by exclusion, by polarity between an absolute assertion and an absolute negation. How did the logic of gradation, a logic that seems much more suitable to the complexity of human affairs, come to be replaced by the logic of exclusion?

Within the human world, the assertion of the primacy of a certain good does not entail the total exclusion of other goods; on the contrary, it only implies that they are recognized as somewhat inferior goods. If, however, one compares the human world as a whole with the religious world, the question is no longer what *element* of the human world must command, but which *world*—human or divine—must command. But how can these two incomparable worlds, the human and the divine, be "compared"? They are incomparable because each of them, in a different way, is self-sufficient. Within a human city-state, the pretensions of wealth cannot ignore those of liberty, nor can they completely ignore those of wisdom. But the priest, who reveals God's truth and heals sin through the sacrament, has little in common with the citizen who defends the rights of wealth, or freedom, or even wisdom.

Therefore the human and the religious worlds cannot be compared, and yet it is necessary to decide between their respective claims. If peace is at last to be achieved, a *third world* must be constructed, one where the conflict will lose all urgency because it will lose its meaning. But constructing a new world does not seem within man's power. What is to be done? If the two worlds are in conflict, it is because they are in contact. In this sense, they do have something in common. This common ground, the locus of their conflict, is man himself. Not man as member of the human city (since the church claims him), nor man as faithful member of the Church (since the human city claims him), but the man who belongs to neither of these two cities. This man's name is already known to us: he is the *individual*.

Of course, the individual does not exist as such. Each "individual" is always already a member of a human city and also a believer within a church. But insofar as he is needed by both realms, each of which wants to snatch him away from the other, he belongs to neither one; he exists as "individual." In other words, the individual "exists" insofar as he hesitates in his obedience and is considered "prior to" his choice of obedience. Since all men are the target of the twofold claim of which I am speaking, all of them can be considered as individuals. It can be objected that this is a purely abstract point of view, leaving the reality of the conflict intact. But if, starting from this *idea* of the individual, I succeed in conceiving of a viable political *institution,* then this inexistent individual will come into existence as citizen or subject of this institution. If that is possible, we will have created this third world which appeared to be beyond our grasp.

To fulfill its function, this new political institution by its very constitution must prevent the individual from being claimed by either the old city or the old Church. The obedience to which the individual will be subjected must be invulnerable to the criticisms and claims of the former candidates for power. They are the candidates of the human city—virtue, riches, liberty—as well as those of the divine city—the law or grace which comes from God, the doctrine revealed by Him, and the men who take their inspiration from this doctrine. The particularity of the new obedience is that it will be indisputable in principle. Of course, one will continue to hear the old claims, those of the rich, the poor, the wise, the priests. But their impact will be blunted by the absolute character of the obedience founding the new city. They will be *neutralized.* The new political institution will envelop and surmount the old conflict which seemed insoluble. The conflict will undoubtedly survive but in domesticated form, confined to the subpolitical level of "society."

Let us imagine then that all men are individuals, that is, men prior to obedience. Let us imagine the state of nature. In this state, men are not subjected to the prestige of wise men, the seductions of the rich, the intimidations of the strong, the preaching of priests; prior to any secular or religious society, they are equal and free. The body politic that they would form from this condition would be necessarily invulnerable to the claims of the rich as well as those of the poor, those of the strong as well as those of the priests. None of these categories would inspire the foundation of the institution, thus none of them would enter into its essential constitution.

What I have just tried to suggest is the raison d'être of the state of nature in Hobbes's work. It is the key notion of political reflection, one that will remain crucial for more than a century, during the formative period of modern liberal regimes. The state of nature is the condition of men before any obedience to the city-state or Church, a condition from which it is possible to construct a body politic invulnerable to the conflict between state and Church. Certainly, in Hobbes's doctrine, the state of nature does not appear as a mere hypothesis needed by the project of surmounting the conflict between politics and religion, but as the reality produced by the actual conflict: the war of all against all. This is why Hobbes prefers the expression *natural* condition of mankind to that of "the state of nature." But essentially, the state of nature is *not* a state of war. We are going to observe this in studying Locke and Rousseau. The generating power of Hobbes's doctrine stems from the fact that with him the respective aspects of the hypothesis and reality of the state of nature are indistinguishable. And they have to be if the hypothesis is to be plausible, if the political art to come is to have a support in nature. And yet Hobbes authorizes his successors to distinguish between the two aspects. Once the plausibility and fecundity of the hypothesis are established, the possibility arises for anyone to modify its terms so as to realize better the end for which it was first conceived.

From Hobbes to Locke and Rousseau, the idea of the body politic will amount to absolute sovereignty variously conceived, founded on and deduced from a state of nature. I have tried to show the theologico-political origin of this notion which has become so unfamiliar to us. If it continued to prevail until the end of the eighteenth century, that is because the motive giving it birth remained effective. Here, however, a nuance must be added. For even if Locke and Rousseau were as concerned as Hobbes to abolish religion's political power, even if Rousseau concluded the *Social Contract* by extolling Hobbes for having reduced the duality of political and religious powers to the unity of the civil sovereign, it is still true that their principal enemy was no longer the political power of religion. Rather, it was a phenomenon that seems to be strictly political, namely absolutism. (In Rousseau's case, it was also the social, political, and moral reality of inequality.) Locke and Rousseau do indeed seem to turn against Hobbes, and it is important that we understand why. The fact that they criticize Hobbes for having given arguments to absolutism does not mean that they do not share the intention that led Hobbes to construct his Leviathan. They simply observe that real absolutism, instead of accomplishing Hobbes's intention, actually gets in its way: it is through absolutism or its protection that religion retains political power. Therefore they criticize Hobbes's doctrine in order to carry out his intention more effectively.

At the same time, it is true that the beginning of the implementation of the Hobbesian program—what is called the "rise of absolutism"— induces difficulties unfamiliar to Hobbes's original problem. The "third world" or "third city" had begun to live its own life. Consequently, if this life turned out to be unsatisfactory, it was proof, in Locke's eyes and especially in Rousseau's, that Hobbes's program had been imperfectly conceived. They remained faithful, however, to Hobbes's fundamental instrument, the state of nature; they simply thought that he did not make all possible use of it, that he did not interpret it radically enough. They reckoned that by interpreting it more radically, they would be in a position both to carry Hobbes's program through to a successful conclusion, and to deal with the disadvantages that his program's implementation had begun to reveal.

CHAPTER IV

Locke, Labor, and Property

As WE HAVE SEEN, the reason for the appearance of the state of nature as a key notion of political reflection stemmed from the necessity of producing an incontestable obligation to obey. Perhaps the most striking feature of Leviathan's power is that it is incontestable: its "absolute" or "unlimited" character signifies that in principle no objection to it can be raised. And the central difficulty in Hobbes's doctrine can be formulated as follows: can one define and construct a *human* power in such a way as to make it, in principle and in fact, invulnerable to criticism? Hobbes thinks that he overcomes the difficulty by basing his reasoning on a reality—the fear of violent death—stronger than any reasoning. But then he confronts two major problems.

Hobbes's reasoning ends where it began: with the fear of death. This is the motive for Leviathan's construction and remains the principle of his effectiveness once he is constituted. Ultimately the subjects conduct themselves peacefully because they are afraid of the sovereign. Certainly from Hobbes's perspective, this fear is incomparably more circumscribed than the original fear; far from contradicting the elementary conditions of a decent human life, it *is* its elementary condition. In this regard, one can speak, along with Michael Oakeshott, of "homeopathic" fear. For, if the desire for self-preservation is the source of Leviathan's legitimacy in the state of nature, the fear that Leviathan then inspires, however "homeopathic" it may be, can be the basis of a new legitimacy. This is so true that, according to Hobbes himself, I have the right to preserve my life even against Leviathan's orders, if these orders put my life in danger. In other words, the search for *security* that founds Leviathan's *unlimited* power will subsequently found its *limitation*.

But if it is necessary to start from the state of nature to construct the legitimate political institution, did Hobbes correctly describe that state? Is the state of nature *essentially* a state of war? Certainly civil war is a good approximation of the war of all against all, but is civil war the truth of political life? Or is it only an exceptional circumstance from which nothing can be inferred for organizing "ordinary" social and political life? And can human nature really be reduced to the desire for power? These are ques-

tions that necessarily reintroduce controversy into an approach whose
goal had been to suppress it. All these questions can be summed up in one:
what is truly the "natural condition of mankind," what is "the most
natural in man"? To this question, as we shall see, Locke and Rousseau
will give answers very different from that of Hobbes. But first we have to
see how Hobbes's interpretation of the state of nature elicits its own
refutation.

What is the meaning of the *jus in omnia,* the right over everything, that
belongs to every individual in the state of nature? It means that each
individual is in himself an indivisible whole whose unique rule of conduct
is to preserve his life. But why does the need for self-preservation mean he
has a right over everything? Because, says Hobbes, he is perpetually threatened, actually or potentially, by others, because the relationship linking
him to others is one of hostility. The *jus in omnia* is born from the intersec-
tion of two essentially distinct ideas: the absolute moral independence of
the individual, and his hostile relationship with other individuals. Of these
two ideas, the latter is the more important: it is because hostility is universal that self-preservation is the unique principle of action taken by the
individual. Put in stronger terms, it is because the hostile relationship is
universal that each person is an individual, that is, an indivisible whole
closed in on himself, morally self-sufficient, thinking only of preserving his
life. What is "the most natural" in the "natural condition of mankind" is
not the independent individual as such, it is the war of all against all that
gives him birth. In other words, the individual exists only through a kind of
negative sociability, that of war. The unlimited right he has is only an effect
of this war. Consequently, the individual does not truly have this right; it
appears only when he is threatened by death. In the state of nature it is
continuously possessed, since there the mortal threat is continuous, and it
reappears in the civil state, even against Leviathan, when the mortal threat
arises.

Thus one sees how Hobbes elaborates, with an extraordinary power of
suggestion, a new idea of the body politic: power is an ingenious device
constructed by powerless individuals for protecting their rights. He does
not succeed, however, in carrying out this idea completely. Individuals in
the state of nature are not truly individuals entitled to rights intrinsically
belonging to them, and power constructed in this way is not really a
protector of their rights since it can protect them only insofar as it
threatens them. The program of what later became liberalism is thus laid
out. It will entail giving the Hobbesian idea of political power its full scope
by modifying its beginning and its end. The individual in the state of nature
will acquire intrinsic rights, and power will be limited to the protection of
individual rights. This will be Locke's approach. Locke begins like
Hobbes: the first need and therefore man's fundamental right is that of

preserving his life. But what threatens his life? Locke answers: not other individuals, but rather hunger. This is the original difference between Locke and Hobbes. For the latter, death first threatens in the form of the hostile other man; for the former it threatens in the form of hunger.

Hobbes is remarkably reserved about the role of hunger in the state of nature, even if he mentions as being obvious that in it, men are "poor." The fact of war and its consequences overshadow war's motives, hunger among them. From the moment that fear engenders fear war feeds on itself, and the question of its "origins" indeed appears to be secondary. Hobbes in fact suggests two origins: first, rivalry for the possession of "goods" (rivalry based on "scarcity," "economic" rivalry); then pure rivalry, based on the desire for power, prestige, reputation ("moral," "political," or "spiritual" in origin). In the state of nature, these two types of rivalry are indistinguishable since they have the same effects. If I take my neighbor's herd, it can be to nourish myself or because I want to possess the larger herd. Which of these two versions of rivalry is more important for Hobbes? Apparently the latter: Hobbes explicitly defines the desire for power, the desire to be first, as the fundamental human passion to which the others can be reduced. And yet if one judges by the effect, the former is more important. If men accept Leviathan, it is for guaranteeing their *security*, the condition, Hobbes points out, for all "industry." Accepting Leviathan's "protection," they escape the risks implied by the unending quest for more power. And here we see the moral ambiguity of the Hobbes's vision, which also makes it so bewitching: men defined explicitly as "aristocrats" (struggling for power, honor, or prestige) behave at the decisive moment like "bourgeois" (making certain that their security comes first).

Hobbes's successors will endeavor to remove this ambiguity. Locke, by an elegant simplification, will simply erase rivalry, or at least its original character. In the beginning, there were no relationships among men, not even hostile ones. As for Rousseau, he accepts the Lockean point of view and pushes it even further by making original man a solitary, happy brute. But at the same time he takes Hobbes's "psychology" very seriously. In his *Second Discourse,* he describes how the individual, beginning as a solitary brute, becomes greedy for riches, power, and prestige. To remove the ambiguity of Hobbes's "psychology," he is the first to have recourse to a history. It was left to Hegel to provide the most convincing solution: the motor of historical development lies in the original situation described by Hobbes. The two "moralities" fighting each other in the state of nature lead to the distinction between two types of men: those who prefer prestige to security, and those who prefer security to the risks that the pursuit of prestige entails. What Hegel would later call the "dialectic of the master and slave" is already contained in the Hobbesian state of nature, and in this dialectic all of mankind's history.[1]

The man about whom Locke speaks in his political *Treatises* is simpler and poorer than Hobbesian man. But, as we have seen, this simplification is in a sense authorized by Hobbes himself: the man who makes a contract prefers security to power. One could even say that Lockean man is more Hobbesian than Hobbes's man. The one who is driven by the desire for power is driven by the desire for a specifically human good, even if the pursuit of this "good" has disastrous consequences; the one who is driven by hunger is driven simply by the desire to flee from evil.[2] In simplifying Hobbes, Locke makes him more coherent.

Of course, making Hobbes coherent was not Locke's primary intention. It was rather to attach rights directly to the solitary individual from the state of nature. If man fundamentally is hungry man, he is radically separated from his fellow man; his only relationships are with his body and with nature. If Locke succeeds in basing individual rights solely on hunger, on the relationship of the solitary individual with nature, he will have shown how human rights can be an attribute of the lone individual.

Take then the individual in the state of nature who goes off in search of food.[3] He gathers plums from a tree and eats them. To say that he eats them means that he appropriates them. He has the right to eat them because, if he did not, he would die. This right is thus independent of any consent of other individuals. Locke observes that if everyone had to wait for others' consent to appropriate the fruits of the earth, humanity would have disappeared long ago. Since our man appropriates the plums legitimately, he is legitimately their owner. The decisive question then is the following: at what point does he become their legitimate owner? Answer: when he takes them from the common domain to use them for satisfying his needs; in other words, when he picks them from the tree. What distinguishes the picked plums from those remaining on the tree? The former have been transformed by the *labor* of the individual, who has combined them with the work of his hands. Every man being naturally the owner of his person and hence of his labor, previously common property can become his own because he has mixed his labor with it. He has become its legitimate owner. Property enters the world through labor, and each individual has within himself the greatest source of property; because he is a laborer and owns himself, he is the owner of his labor as well.

Thanks to this simple analysis, Locke established two important propositions. The right to property is essentially prior to the institution of society, independent of others' consent or political law; in other words, the right to property is a right belonging to the lone individual and closely linked to the urgent necessity of nourishing oneself. Property is natural and not conventional. The second proposition is this: the relationship of man to nature is defined by *labor*. Man is not naturally a political animal; he is an *owning* and *laboring* animal, owning because he is laboring, laboring in order to own.

Thus Locke solidly established the right to property. He broke with tradition in making it a strictly individual right. Certainly, tradition considered it as a natural right, but it emphasized the "social" aspect of property, its being regulated by law or social duty. It is true that on this point Locke at first seems to accept a natural limitation to the natural right to property. The right to property in this first stage of the state of nature is, according to Locke, limited by two obligations. On the one hand, I have no right to appropriate more than I can consume, since that would be wasteful. If I gather more plums than I can eat, the ones left over will rot. On the other hand, I must leave some plums for others, so that they can appropriate in their turn the fruits of the earth.

But Locke then abolishes these two limits that he initially posed. As for the first, one cannot exactly speak of an obligation, of a moral or political limit. Gathering fruit to let it rot is simply irrational, absurd conduct. The limit which at first seems moral is in fact a physical one. I have no right to appropriate more than I can consume, simply because I cannot. I do not have the means to do it. Furthermore, anything "appropriated" in this way would not be appropriated but wasted, hence lost. Now, suppose I find a means of avoiding this waste, by agreeing with my fellow men to exchange the naturally corruptible goods for an equivalent of incorruptible ones, for example, gold and silver. Then the accumulation will be limitless because it will no longer involve waste.

As for the second limit, it seems that the difficulty is greater. What actually guarantees that, once I have stripped the plum tree, another plum tree will be available for my neighbor? After all, Hobbes saw in such a rivalry for goods one of the sources of the war of all against all, in which each person has a right over everything and everyone. In response, Locke appears initially to suggest that, in the original state of nature, the fruits of the earth being overabundant, each person could appropriate them for his consumption without wronging others. But that is only a historical hypothesis, and a contestable one at that. Therefore Locke, unlike Rousseau, scarcely insists on it. (For Rousseau this hypothesis will become an essential element in his interpretation of the human condition.) Locke introduces a consideration that changes the terms of the problem: the plums are a less significant form of available property than land. Ownership of land is also born from labor: I am naturally the legitimate owner of the land I cultivate with my labor. Now, tilling the land makes it produce much more than it would produce spontaneously. Therefore, by appropriating a portion of land through labor, far from reducing humanity's common good, I *add* to it: I add the fruits of the earth that owe their existence to my labor. And it is obvious that no one else has a right to these goods, since they are not given by nature but produced by my labor. Locke insists on this point: it is human labor, and not nature, that gives things their *value*. The natural state of nature, so to speak, is not abundance but scarcity.

To sum of Locke's analysis: the individual has a natural right to a property that has no natural limits. It has no natural limits because the invention of money allows us to make any corruptible goods incorruptible, and because the value of things comes from human labor and not from nature's bounty. From this fact, a paradoxical consequence ensues: the right of property is naturally separated from the labor that is at its origin. From the moment that money makes it possible to represent and preserve quantities of labor, the legitimate owner is no longer necessarily the laborer. It suffices that the exchange be free for the property to preserve its value, and thus continue to represent the quantity of labor that it incorporates. For example, an individual who lives from the buying and selling of goods without producing them is a legitimate owner. He robs no one, takes nothing away of value in the society, but rather preserves value, putting it into circulation and making it work and thereby increasing it. Once property, which enters the world through labor, becomes a value represented by money, the owner's right is legitimately separated from the laborer's right.

These two conclusions of Locke's are obviously of great importance for the elaboration of liberal doctrine and deserve reflection. Let us look first at the invention of money. It is, by definition, an agreement. The origin of this agreement is the natural desire of the individual who wants to make the goods he has produced, and is incapable of consuming, incorruptible, in order to exchange them for other consumer goods which he needs. This desire is linked to the desire for preservation and is an ingenious device for satisfying it more completely. At the same time, it implies a relationship between the individuals who conclude the agreement: it is a kind of contract. Thus one sees being born from nature a *society*, a series of regulated relationships among individuals. In Locke's interpretation, "society," or at least its essential elements, is born before the political institution. I have mentioned that Hobbes had already elaborated the distinction between civil society and the state, or between civil society and political society. But his "civil society" is originally founded on a negative sociability, that of war. Prior to the political institution, it is essentially unbearable. With Locke, it becomes bearable. Society becomes the series of economic exchanges into which men enter as laborers and owners. The Lockean state of nature is both more individualistic and more social than that of Hobbes. Rights, in the form of the fundamental right to property, belong to the solitary individual, and this individual builds up positive relationships with others.

Locke's second conclusion concerns the delicate problem of the relationship of the individual, labor, and property. At the start, labor and property are closely linked in their common source, the individual. My labor is mine because I am the owner of my person, and my property is mine because it has its origin in my labor. Labor and property are related to each other in a circular way; at the center of this circle is the individual. But Locke is very precise: labor is only the beginning of ownership. Eventually, labor is separated from ownership. More precisely, the right to property is separated from the worker's right to the fruits of his labor.

Is the laborer's right infringed, then? Not at all, Locke answers. The peculiarity of labor is not to produce the right to property, it is to produce value. The distinctive feature of property is to preserve this value, to prevent it from disappearing or being wasted. This value is best preserved when its preservation is an extension of the individual's desire for preservation. In other words, when he does not discuss the origin of property, Locke considers labor as "disindividualized," as the quantity of social labor as a whole. If property is separated from the laborer, it is not the laborer who is robbed, it is the value of labor that is preserved.

In other words, in the beginning, the owner's right and the laborer's are one and the same. But once the invention of money and the development of trade make it possible for labor to be productive, to produce more than is necessary for the producer's consumption, owner and laborer become distinct. The right to property remains an individual right, the laborer's right becoming the right of work to see its product preserved, which can be done only through the individual right to property. And the laborer's right is not infringed since according to Locke, the condition of an agricultural laborer, in a society thus defined by labor's productivity and the individual right to property, is more comfortable than that of an Indian king in America. Locke begins with a strictly individualistic and moral justification of property rights and ends with a collective and utilitarian one. The final justification of the right to property is its economic utility.

What Locke has made us see is the development of economic society from its modest beginning in the hungry individual. All economic life, including trade, labor's productivity, and the right to property, takes on the natural and incontestable character of the hungry individual's right to nourish himself. In this hungry individual lies the primordial basis of human life. One sees why the liberal program, once completely elaborated, made the right to property and the economy in general the foundation of social life. Although the rules organizing social life must be born strictly from the right of the solitary individual, they can find their foundation only in the relationship of this individual to nature. Simultaneously, the relationship of the individual's labor to nature conjures up a world essentially distinct from that of the individual's rights: the world of value, of the productivity of labor, of utility. From the second point of view, the right to property is no longer considered man's fundamental natural right. it is simply the means of preserving the values that result from labor's productivity, the means of production and the exchange of values.

After Locke's time, and in large part thanks to him, the right to property was recognized as *the* fundamental natural right. When it no longer had to play this role, attention focused on this second aspect. The economy appeared less the product of solitary individuals asserting their rights, and more the "system" of production and exchange of values, "the system of political economy." And the determining notion of political economy ceased to be the absolute right of the individual, becoming an essentially relative notion, interest or utility. Locke embodies that moment when liberalism became fully aware of its foundation in the individual right to property. At the same time, he made it possible to understand how the liberal philosophy of natural right spontaneously transformed itself into an entirely different type of thought: political economy.

I pointed out earlier the great difference separating Aristotle's approach from that of Hobbes. Aristotle reached his conclusion at the end of a long discussion that represents a refinement of political discussion such as it must have occurred spontaneously in the city-state. As for Hobbes, he aims at reaching a result that is not only true but also essentially incontestable, since it is based on something stronger than any discursive reasoning: fear of death. It is important to point out here that Locke's approach is just as "absolutist" as Hobbes's. The original right of each person is essentially above discursive reasoning, above any objection, because it is based on a solitary and silent activity: labor for consumption. In Locke's eyes, the meaning of justice can only be to guarantee property. It is absurd to doubt the justice of property rights, since the very idea of justice presupposes ownership. Those who object to this right, or who demand the consent of the body politic for this right to be a true one, are disdainfully dismissed as "quarrelers and quibblers"; they simply want to deprive others of the fruit of their labor. And Locke notes that it is certain that the world was not given to such people, but only to those who are "rational and industrious."

Hobbes had noted that civil war is often born from uncertainty and from conflict over what is "right" or "legitimate" or "just." The absolute sovereign neutralizes this conflict by identifying what is "just" with what is declared so by the sovereign. Locke neutralizes it in a more economic way. Since individual property is the basis of justice, and since property in its origin requires no relationship among men, justice cannot be the object of a genuine uncertainty, and hence of rational debate. Justice is *always already realized,* as long as property is guaranteed and protected. The only conceivable discussion of justice is identical with a debate fixing the rate of exchange of properties on the market, a debate whose outcome is always "just" since it is based on the consent of the two parties. It must be admitted that an author like Hayek is loyal to liberalism's original inspiration in claiming that the notion of "social justice" makes no sense.

These remarks help us to understand why economic activity became the dominant activity in liberal societies, more precisely why the erection of the "sovereign state" above "civil society" corresponded to the liberation of economic activity and, soon, its dominant position in society. We have seen that the sovereign state, in having the means and the right to demand total obedience, tends to neutralize the secular as well as the religious motives that drive men to acquire power and influence over each other. But this sovereignty constitutes only the exterior framework of men's actions. Assuming that they obey, what *else* are they going to do in civil society? In what terms are they going to relate to each other? The same movement that brings the sovereign state to forbid men to exercise personal power over each other is going to lead the members of society to turn progressively away from each other, to avoid encounters in which they experience mortal dangers. They are going to seek a neutral ground for their actions, one where they do not meet their fellow men and where they do not encroach upon sovereignty. Up to the constitution of the sovereign state, the primary object of each person's action was the other man. Henceforth, that object will be *nature*. Men turn away from men and instead turn themselves toward nature so as to understand and control it. Science is neutral and its conclusions are imposed on everyone. It is above the particular interests and partisan passions of men, not unlike the sovereign, at least in principle. The economy, closely linked with science, tends to become the arena par excellence of human activity because, in its finality, the economy is directed toward nature and not toward other men. The development of absolute sovereignty within the framework of the state, and the development of science and economy within the framework of civil society, have the same motivating force. I have indicated how Locke's philosophical viewpoint prepared the "scientific" viewpoint of political economy. The fact remains, however, that Locke stopped well short of the latter. In his doctrine, the world of the economy alone is not sufficient, it needs the political institution for guaranteeing its existence. On this fundamental point, Locke remains within Hobbes's schema.

We have already observed that the Lockean state of nature is not a state of war. Locke had to distinguish between them if he wanted to avoid the despotic or absolutist consequences of Hobbes's doctrine, if he wanted to attach rights to a truly solitary individual. But here a difficulty immediately arises. If the state of nature is not a state of war, if in it men can become proprietors, developing production and trade, why would they ever leave it? To what need would the political institution respond? Here, moreover, we find the principal difficulty of the notion of the state of nature. The more "satisfying" it is, the "happier" it is, then the more likely it is to provide the image of natural rights that the political institution should guarantee and protect; but simultaneously, it becomes less clear why men left this state to enter into a body politic. The better it fills the political function for which one imagined it, the more it makes the political institution superfluous.

Locke gets out of the difficulty by asserting that although the state of nature is not essentially a state of war, it tends naturally to become so. In the state of nature, men have no recognized judges to arbitrate their differences: each one is judge of his own cause. Consequently, everyone's rights are in perpetual danger. The state of nature always ends up becoming a state of war. This is the "Hobbesian moment" of the Lockean doctrine. And any doctrine of the state of nature and the social contract (even Rousseau's) necessarily has a Hobbesian moment, since only an unbearable state of war, an intolerable evil can explain why men agreed to leave a state where in principle their rights were flourishing. But this Hobbesian moment is not satisfactorily solved in Hobbes's own system. In contrast, the Lockean solution can be seen as having been aimed directly against Hobbes's.[4] Locke's objection is well known: transmitting all of one's rights to an absolute sovereign does not mean leaving the state of war, it only makes it worse. Under the guise of fabricating a protector, one arms an enemy. To protect oneself from foxes (one's neighbors), one puts oneself in the clutches of a lion. Some other solution must be sought.

In the state of nature, each person is the sole judge of transgressions of the law of nature. To leave this state, a common definition of these transgressions must be agreed on, just as there must be agreement on the laws defining them, laws that state clearly what is *yours* and what is *mine*. If the laws are to be effective, they must apply equally to everyone, nobody must be exempt (and especially not the "sovereign"). If they are not to be oppressive, each person must be able to contribute to their conception and promulgation, singly or through representatives. To leave the state of nature, or enter into "civil society," is essentially to constitute a *legislative assembly*.[5]

The purpose of the political institution is to preserve property endangered by the inevitable disorders of the state of nature. To leave this state, it is necessary to institute a "supreme power" that has the right to demand obedience; simultaneously, so that this power cannot willfully divest members of their property and liberty, it must itself be subjected to the laws it enacts. Only a representative and sovereign legislative body fulfills this double condition, and only as long as certain precautions are taken. For example, it must not remain continuously assembled, since then its own interests would risk becoming distinct from the common interest. But even though the legislative body should not be continuously convened, the laws must be continuously applied. Hence the necessity of another power, subordinate to the first, the *executive* power. Since all the circumstances of governmental action cannot be foreseen or encompassed by laws, this latter power must be left sufficient latitude for confronting imponderables, and for adapting the laws themselves to what the public good requires. The executive must be granted a *prerogative*. Executive power, in its principal definition, enforces the laws; its sphere of action is within the body politic. A third power is therefore needed, which itself can hardly be regulated by laws. This power responsible for foreign relations, for peace and war, Locke calls the *federative* power, adding that for reasons of convenience it is most often in the hands of the executive.[6]

Despite the impression of clarity that this summary undoubtedly gives, Locke's theory of powers is not easy to understand. One must make the effort, however, because the functioning of modern democracies is in the end determined by the relations between legislative and executive power, and by its apparent clarity. One is tempted to understand this distinction in the light of the later doctrine of "separation of powers." In reality, it is difficult to place Locke's theory under this latter rubric. Although he contributed greatly to elaborating this latter doctrine, it should be said that Locke makes its difficulties highly perceptible to us. According to him, in any body politic fulfilling its mission of protecting property, there is *one* "supreme" power which no political will, no constituted power has the right to oppose. That is the legislative power. As such, this power is as "absolute" as Hobbes's Leviathan. Executive power is *derived* from and essentially *subordinated* to it: it is its instrument. Between the two, there is a considerable difference of political dignity, of moral consistency. It is true that the executive has its "prerogative," but its existence is due less to the intrinsic dignity of the executive than to the necessities of social and political life. Locke recognizes in the executive only a de facto weight and importance, but not a de jure dignity. This inequality between the principle and the fact sums up the Lockean executive problem, which is also the problem of the modern executive. Its meaning and legitimacy are uncertain, because modern political legitimacy is based on representation, and because the natural place for national representation is the legislative body. What then is the modern executive?

We must first observe that unlike the legislative power, it is a radically new notion in the history of political thought.[7] Let us consider, for example, book 4 of Aristotle's *Politics*, in which it was thought that an outline of "separation" or "distribution" of powers could be found. Aristotle distinguishes the body that deliberates, the magistrates, and the judiciary power: that is, he distinguishes something resembling the legislative, the executive, and the judiciary. But it is striking that Aristotle's "executive," so to speak, is a plural power, while the modern executive is essentially an indivisible power. We are governed by *one* government, whereas the Greeks or Romans were ruled by *several* magistrates. The mystery of the modern executive is the mystery of its unity.

If this mystery most often goes unnoticed, the reason is simple: it is historical. The modern executive is thought to have taken over from the monarchical power. Locke's and Montesquieu's classical interpretations of the relationship between the executive and legislative appear to be born from the observation of the conflict between the king of England and the House of Commons. But why have all modern democratic republics kept or even created a "monarchical" type of executive? Why in particular did the American republic, which did not replace a native monarchy, endow itself deliberately with what the framers of the Constitution called an "energetic" executive, which was perceived by opponents of the Constitution as dangerously "monarchical"?[8]

Consider how Locke defined the origin and function of the two powers. They both have their source in the state of nature; they are two powers held by every individual living in this state. The legislative is the power of each person to do what he deems best for his preservation and that of others, a power that he is going to abandon partially when he enters into "civil society" so as to be ruled by laws. The executive is the power that each person has, in the state of nature, to punish infractions against the law of nature. When he enters civil society, the individual turns over this power wholly to society. The natural force that the individual in the state of nature could use as he wished to punish transgressors can no longer be used except according to the instructions of the legislative power.[9] The executive force of society is made by combining the executive forces of individuals.

Thus the "political" legislative power is the direct extension of the "natural" legislative power. It is the same power, now limited according to law. The individual, instead of simply doing what seems best for preserving his life, now does what seems best within the limits fixed by the law which, through his representatives, he has contributed to formulating and promulgating. Legislative power is the direct extension of the individual's desire for self-preservation. And it is sovereign or "supreme" because it directly expresses the desire for preserving property, the origin of the political institution.

Executive power is a different matter. Like the legislative, it is present in the state of nature; but unlike it, it is in principle totally abandoned by the individual to the political institution. It can be completely relinquished without harming the individual's rights because, unlike the legislative, it does not express directly the desire for the individual's preservation. Its dignity is entirely subordinated to the legislative body. But this total abandonment proves in fact to be impossible: the individual retains the natural executive power insofar as the law can never be completely effective.[10] Thus, while the civil legislative power extends the natural legislative by making it representative, the natural executive power, which is not representable, can only be abandoned in principle or retained as it is. The civil executive reveals that nature is irreducible to the representative convention. In this sense, it suggests a certain identity between the state of nature and the civil state in Locke's doctrine. But simultaneously, it testifies that the preservation of the body politic is irreducible to the preservation of its members such as the legislative body represents it and inscribes it in laws. Locke's intention was to found the supremacy of the legislative. But his theory of executive power reveals the difference between man's natural and political conditions. The law expresses or represents natural man's desire for preserving his life, but the civil executive, by showing the inadequacy of law, indicates the rupture between the state of nature and the civil state. More than the legislative power, the executive embodies the essence of man's political condition.

Locke thus testifies involuntarily to the ambiguity characterizing the relationship between the two powers in modern times. The legislative, as the more direct expression of individuals in civil society, is the supreme power. Our political institutions founded on the idea of representation naturally attribute supreme power to the legislative power. Simultaneously, executive power embodying the difference between the state and civil society, or between man's political and natural conditions, finds in its de jure inferiority a de facto principle of action. Insofar as it does not represent individuals in their "natural" condition, it will be able to claim to "represent" them in their political condition. The executive will be able to say, for example, that whereas the legislative body represents the "interests of society," it represents the "greatness of the nation."

Thus one can see why the energetic executive is not essentially a monarchical inheritance, but is born naturally from the dialectic between the idea of representation and man's political condition. It embodies the "transcendence" of political power in relation to society—hence the imperious necessity for its unity. The legislative body, owing to its representative character, and in spite of the convention considering the majority's will the will of the body, cannot suffice to incarnate the members' political unity. After all, it is meant to reflect faithfully the diversity of interests and opinions. Certainly one can object that although society's diversities are expressed in the legislative debates, they are also crystallized into a few broad tendencies reflecting the common interest. The majority decision can thus truly be the decision of all, and not just by convention. It is quite true that the legislative body has often been the eminent place of deliberation, that as such it can embody the political unity of society. However, care must be taken to ensure that the representative character of the modern legislative body does not seriously limit the scope of its own deliberations: unlike those of the Athenian Assembly or the Roman Senate, its deliberations can lead only to laws and not to actions. Voting a law always falls decisively short of deciding on an action. Because the modern representative body confines itself to the law and leaves action to the executive, its deliberation is always radically incomplete. The immediate link between deliberation and action is a necessary condition for political action, and more generally for all human action. And since the unity of deliberation and action cannot reside in the legislative body, it will come forth in the executive power. One can truly deliberate only on what must be decided by oneself; one can decide wisely only on what one has oneself deliberated.

These few remarks on the question of the executive have not been aimed against Locke. I simply wished to show how much the idea of political representation, first formulated by Locke in terms that have remained our own, was uncertain and even confused, in spite of its apparent lucidity. I wished to suggest that politics is irreducible to representation, and that the modern emancipation of the executive, contrary to Locke's wishes yet authorized by his doctrine, bears witness to this irreducibility. And since political liberalism rests historically on the idea of representation, this tension between politics and representation will necessarily emerge in any attempt to define a liberal politics.

CHAPTER V

Montesquieu and
the Separation of Powers

In going from Hobbes and Locke to Montesquieu we change worlds. Montesquieu's political intentions remain essentially the same as those of Hobbes and Locke, but the means chosen for realizing them, and the language in which they are described, are radically different.

The political intention remains the same: the end of the political institution is to ensure the *security* of persons and goods. The more certain the security, the more recommendable the institution. But the need for individual self-preservation is no longer strictly speaking the foundation of political legitimacy, of an absolute and incontestable legitimacy. Whereas Hobbes and Locke spoke the language of absolute rights—the individual's or the sovereign's—Montesquieu abandons this language and reestablishes on new bases the flexibility of the ancient politics. For example, Locke considered absolute monarchy to be not only a bad and illegitimate regime, but in fact not a political regime at all. It left men in a state of nature worse than the original one. Montesquieu, in contrast, considered the defects and merits of the French monarchy with equanimity. The French monarchy's principle of legitimacy was radically illiberal, but its effective functioning assured tolerable liberties. In short, Montesquieu's liberalism is not aggressive like Locke's; he is liberal not only in his principles, but also in his mood or tone. If he was able to abandon the Lockean "absolutist" language, it is because he managed to found liberty on bases other than the concepts of the state of nature and sovereignty.

The doctrine of sovereignty was both the salvation and the bane of early modern political thought. It saved it by making possible the conception of a neutral power, superior in principle to all interests and passions that drive men to war, whether political or religious. Sovereignty was responsible for constituting a human world invulnerable in principle to religion's power. The bane was that, by constructing a power capable of imposing peace, one simultaneously raised a power capable of making war on its subjects. Of course, Locke attempted to make it impossible for the absolute sovereignty to turn against citizens by placing it in a legislative assembly representing their desire for preservation. But what if this assembly betrays its mandate, becomes oppressive? Then, says Locke, the only recourse is to appeal to Heaven—to rebel. This recourse is always open since the people are the ultimate source of all legitimacy.[1] Montesquieu will show how the liberal plan can do without the dangerous means of absolute sovereignty, as well as the perilous remedy of rebellion, without risking anarchy.

Unlike Hobbes, Locke makes a *distinction* between the legislative and executive powers but does not achieve a doctrine of the *separation* of powers comparable to Montesquieu's. On the contrary, Locke insists on the essential subordination of the executive to the legislative. For a more or less equal distribution of power between the two cannot be conceived of, so long as sovereignty resides in the king. If the king is sovereign, he must necessarily possess the two powers—or at least, possessing the executive, he must also have a direct share in legislation. The liberal plan therefore required that the idea of royal sovereignty be refuted. To an absolute sovereignty, however, one can oppose only another absolute sovereignty: to that of the king, that of the people. The people's sovereignty, as absolute, is not in principle more propitious to the separation of powers than the king's sovereignty. But since the sovereign people cannot rule directly, and since the assembly of its representatives is also scarcely suited to govern, a regime based on the people's sovereignty practically needs a power other than that of the sovereign. At least Locke's English contemporaries thought so: the Lockean assertion of the people's sovereignty expressed itself practically, at the time of the Glorious Revolution of 1688–89, through a compromise between the representative Houses and the reformed monarchy. Once this compromise was established and began functioning passably well, it became possible to describe English politics as resting on the interplay of two almost equal powers, leaving aside the absolute sovereignty that had made the compromise possible, and leaving the question of legitimacy to lie dormant.

Montesquieu's doctrine is not founded on an analysis of man's original condition or of the bases of political legitimacy. It depends on the interpretation of a political experience, namely the English experience, whose results Montesquieu contemplated from afar. The doctrine of the separation of powers finds its classical expression in Montesquieu thanks only to the "forgetting" of the principle of legitimacy that made it possible. Montesquieu's "forgetting," which only reproduced that of English actors and authors who had already made the compromise, suggested that in the future the principle of legitimacy—the people's sovereignty—which made the separation of powers possible, could be turned against it. The two doctrines have no intrinsic affinity: democratic legitimacy, the condition for liberal institutions in the framework of the English monarchy, could in

Power ↑ Liberty

other circumstances become their enemy. Thus Montesquieu's thought represents that unique, exquisite moment of liberalism when the question of legitimacy could be forgotten, a pause between the active sovereignty of kings (which comes to an end with the English Revolution) and the active sovereignty of the people (which begins with the French Revolution).

By seeing the heart of the political problem in the conflict between *power* and *liberty*, Montesquieu determines the definitive language of liberalism. In so doing, he reverses Locke's point of view, so as to carry out the latter's intention more effectively. Instead of starting with the right that founds liberty, he starts with power that threatens it; instead of pondering the origin of power, he ponders its effects. He is doubtless the first author to speak of power as a *thing*, separable in right and fact from its origin as well as its end, man himself. He takes us then to the end of the process that led the modern mind to conceive the ways in which men influence each other under the single concept of "power." The Romans, by contrast, had distinguished at least three forms of political power: *auctoritas, potestas, imperium*. Later Hobbes simplified matters when he reduced all human passions and motives to the desire for power. "The passions that most of all cause the differences of Wit, are principally, the more or lesse Desire of Power, of Riches, of Knowledge, and of Honor. All of which may be reduced to the first, that is Desire for Power. For Riches, Knowledge and Honor are but severall sorts of Power."[2] And again: "So that in the first place, I put for a generall inclination of all mankind, a perpetual and restlesse desire of Power, that ceaseth only in death."[3]

The modification to which Montesquieu subjects Hobbes's teaching is contained in the following phrases: "The natural impulse or desire which Hobbes attributes to mankind of subduing one another is far from being well founded. The idea of empire and dominion is so complex, and depends on so many other notions, that it could never be the first which occurred to the human understanding."[4] And then: "Constant experience shows us that every man *invested with power* is apt to abuse it."[5] In other words, the desire for power is not essentially inscribed in man's nature. It is not born from itself, so to speak, or at least it is born in its excessive and dangerous form only if the individual is in a social or political institution already endowing him with a certain power. It is born thanks to institutions. Consequently a judicious institutional arrangement will make it possible to avoid the abuses of power.

How? Montesquieu's answer is well known: "To prevent this abuse, it is necessary from the very nature of *things* that power should be a check to power."[6] Human nature is sufficiently flexible, sufficiently plastic, for its behavior to be largely determined by the institution in which it lives. No need then of an absolute power to subdue an essentially ambitious and rebellious human will by the death threat, as Hobbes believed; this neu-

Power ↑ institutions

tralizing power can itself be neutralized by being judiciously divided in such a way that one power will be opposed to another. Hobbes was not yet liberal because he saw in man something that rebelled against association and cooperation; Rousseau, despite his hatred of absolutism, was not any more liberal because he saw a basic incompatibility between man's nature and social life, even in a liberal regime. Although he often seems to recall Hobbes and to announce Rousseau, Montesquieu is convinced by the English example that it is possible to bring into harmony man's desires and political necessities by a judicious adjustment of power and liberty: by the "distribution of powers." The account of the distribution of powers is found in the chapter of *The Spirit of the Laws,* (11.6) entitled "Of the Constitution of England." I am going to consider it briefly.

What must be grasped is that Montesquieu is really considering *two* powers, the legislative and the executive. Of course he makes a general distinction among three powers: these two and the judiciary power. But judiciary power has real political importance only in regimes where the first two powers are confused: "Most kingdoms in Europe enjoy a moderate government because the prince who is invested with the two first powers leaves the third to his subjects. In Turkey, where these three powers are united in the Sultan's person, the subjects groan under the most dreadful oppression." In the English regime, as interpreted by Montesquieu, judiciary power does not exist as such: there it is "exercised by persons taken from the body of the people."[7] He comments: "By this method the judicial power, so terrible to mankind, not being annexed to any particular state or profession, becomes, as it were, invisible. People have not then the judges continually present to their view; they fear the office, but not the magistrate." Montesquieu considers this point so important that he (who never repeats himself) repeats it two pages later: "Of the three powers above mentioned, the judiciary is in some measure next to nothing: there remain, therefore, only two."

How does Montesquieu conceive of these two powers and their relationship? He begins by going back to Locke's doctrine on the subordination of the executive to the legislative: the latter contains "the general will of the state," the former, "the execution of that general will." As for the significance of the legislative, it also echoes English philosophy: "As in a country of liberty, every man who is supposed a free agent ought to be his own governor; the legislative power should reside in the whole body of the people. But since this is impossible in large states, and in small ones is subject to many inconveniences, it is fit the people should transact by their representatives what they cannot transact by themselves."

In spite of these superficial resemblances, the accent is going to be very different from that found in Locke. Locke insisted on the continuity, so to speak, between the mass of the people and the body of representatives, on the latter's necessary faithfulness to the trust placed in them. Montesquieu does not contradict this, but insists rather more on what *distinguishes* the representative body from the mass of the people. The faithfulness of the representatives to the electorate is valuable only if they also know how to be unfaithful; one has the feeling that the principal merit of representation is to prevent the people from taking "active resolutions," "something of which it is entirely incapable." In Montesquieu's eyes, the people are entirely capable of choosing their representatives well, but not of deliberating well: deliberation must be left to the representatives. One sees how, from Locke to Montesquieu, the interest moves from the origin of power toward its exercise or functioning.

As for the executive power, it "must be in a monarch's hands," because this post of government is technically better administrated by a single person rather than by several. Yet the principle of this monarch's legitimacy, the origin of his power, are never discussed. Decidedly, the interest is elsewhere. The most important concern is obviously the relationship between the two powers. Here again, Montesquieu's emphasis is contrary to Locke's. For Montesquieu, the danger for liberty comes rather from the legislative body:

> Were the executive power not to have a right of restraining the encroachments of the legislative body, the latter would become despotic; for as it might arrogate to itself what authority it pleased, it would soon destroy all the other powers. But it is not proper, on the other hand, that the legislative power should have a right to stay the executive. For as the execution has its natural limits, it is useless to confine it; besides, the executive power is generally employed in momentary operations.

And although of course the legislative must have the possibility of examining how the laws have been carried out, it cannot judge the conduct of the person who carries them out; his person must be "sacred." Finally, in legislative matters, the monarch must have the option, if not of making rulings, at least of "preventing" them.

Montesquieu perceives very clearly that in a regime based on representation the legislative body, as holder of representative legitimacy, is the most naturally tempted to increase its power abusively. Hence, precautions must be taken to ensure a sufficient consistency to the executive. The end of all constitutional provisions is to make the two powers approximately equal in strength, or capacities, even though in accordance with the principle of the regime's legitimacy, the executive should be strictly subordinate to the legislative. The question then is obviously the following: are not these two equal powers going to paralyze each other? Hobbes would not have failed to notice that putting two equal powers opposite each other is a sure recipe for instituting permanent war between them. One must submit to the other or their conflict will bring on the ruin of the body politic. Montesquieu judges it otherwise: "These three powers (including the Upper House) should naturally form a state of repose or inaction. But as there is a necessity for movement in the course of human affairs, they are forced to move, but still in concert."

The classic objection of the absolutists is that somebody has to decide in the last resort, and the one who does necessarily enjoys absolute sovereignty. Montesquieu agrees that these decisions must be made, but denies that they must be taken by *one* power. *One* decision can be taken by *two* powers that have agreed; and they will agree (*volens nolens*) precisely because a decision must be made. The true sovereign of such a regime is neither the legislative nor the executive, but necessity. Most of the decisions taken will not have been desired by either of the two powers. Montesquieu even speaks in his papers of a "miraculous bill" that "passed against the will of the Commons, the Lords and king."

Given that decisions must be made and that therefore the two powers are forced to agree, will they not possibly agree on something to the detriment of the citizens? Might they not reach an agreement to oppress them, to divide up their spoils? What Montesquieu suggests is that the compromise between the two powers will take place necessarily, or at least generally, to the benefit of the citizen's liberty. The explanation of this fortunate result is found in another chapter of *The Spirit of the Laws,* which is as important as the one we have just considered, but too often is neglected by commentators. While chapter 6 of book 11 describes the statics of the separation of powers, chapter 27 of book 19 reveals its dynamics. It introduces a fundamental notion for understanding the functioning of free regimes, the notion of *party:*

> As there are in this state two visible powers—the legislative and executive— and as every citizen has a will of his own, and may at pleasure assert his independence, most men have a greater fondness for one of these powers than for the other, and the multitude have commonly neither equity nor sense enough to show an equal affection to both.
>
> And as the executive power, by disposing of all employments, may give great hopes, and no fears, every man who obtains any favor from it is ready to espouse its cause; while it is liable to be attacked by those who have nothing to hope from it.
>
> All the passions being unrestrained, hatred, envy, jealousy, and an ambitious desire of riches and honors, appear in their extent; were it otherwise, the state would be in the condition of a man weakened by sickness, who is without passions because he is without strength.
>
> The hatred which arises between *two parties* will always subsist, because it will always be *impotent.*

These parties being composed of freemen, if the one becomes too powerful for the other, as *a consequence of liberty* this other is depressed; while the citizens take the weaker side, with the same readiness as the hands lend their assistance to remove the infirmities and disorders of the body.

Every individual is independent, and being commonly led by caprice and humor, frequently changes parties; he abandons one where he left all his friends, to unite himself to another in which he finds all his enemies: so that in this nation it frequently happens that the people forget the laws of friendship, as well as those of hatred. (emphasis added)

I must attempt to analyze briefly this very remarkable text, in which the extraordinarily evocative description of the England of Walpole and Bolingbroke prophetically contains a summary of the functioning of two centuries of representative regime.

Each of the two powers, precisely because it confronts another power of approximately equal strength, needs partisans. And because it is a power, it is bound to attract them. Just as power is divided in two, society is going to be divided between the partisans of one power and those of the other. The citizens are going to wish themselves represented by one or the other: even the executive is going to become representative in a way. The citizens are going to seek to realize their ends through the power they favor and whose favor they hope to win. But their will cannot have an immediate or direct effect, since it can be realized only through a power that is held in respect by another power. Because society is represented by a divided power, the citizens are going to be powerless to do much to harm each other.

But what if one of the parties is supported by such a large majority that it obliterates the other party and the citizens who support it? Montesquieu responds by referring to the *consequence of liberty*. If one of the powers seems to get carried away, he argues, then the citizens will go to the aid of the other. But why is he so certain that such a mechanism will come into play? Why does he think that citizens will divide into two almost equal parties corresponding to the two powers?

Citizens are certainly partisans of one or the other power and hope to gain advantages from it. But above all they are members of society, which is distinguished from the two powers. Consequently, if one of the powers takes too much advantage, a certain number of its own partisans, the most lukewarm at first, will feel threatened as members of society. Actually, citizens have a twofold interest: that the power serve their interest, *and* that it not weigh too heavily on society. They also have a twofold feeling: that the power they favor "represents" them, *and* also that it is different from them—that it does not understand or will betray them. It is the inevitable interplay of these two inseparable interests and feelings that guarantees that the citizens will spontaneously help the weaker power. The "double dealing" of citizens with power is inscribed in the logic of representation: from the moment that power is supposed to represent the citizen, the feeling of alienation grows along with the desire for identification.

Thus such a regime produces a double impotence. The division of power leaves the citizens generally incapable of doing much to each other; conversely, citizens can easily make the power powerless by changing parties.[8] The impotence of citizens and of power condition each other. This is ultimately what Montesquieu calls *liberty*. Since divided power can neither do much against the citizen (hence the feeling of security), nor for him (except for patronage) the citizen has only to "assert his independence whenever he pleases." He turns his desires and activities toward domains unfamiliar to politics, toward domains where strictly speaking one does not exercise power over other men. He can now earn money or write books: the economy and culture are the two great domains liberated by this double impotence.

Liberty is produced through the neutralization of the political. But it should not be said that this liberty is apolitical; it is a liberty conditioned by the political organization which neutralizes the power of power. Hence, in a free regime, the citizens "assert their independence whenever they please." It would certainly seem that liberty and independence are the same thing. However, in chapter 3 of book 11, entitled "In What Liberty Consists," Montesquieu warns that "political liberty does not consist in an unlimited freedom. . . . We must have continually present to our minds the difference between independence and liberty. Liberty is a right of doing whatever the law permits." To understand Montesquieu's thought on this crucial point, we must reconcile two of his apparently contradictory assertions. On the one hand, in a free regime, citizens are independent; on the other, political liberty does not consist in being independent but in being able to do whatever the *laws* allow. But what if the law forbids everything or almost everything? The solution to the contradiction is found in Montesquieu's conception of the law. In a free regime founded on the separation of powers, laws will necessarily tend to "permit" citizens a great number of things, widening the sphere of their "independence." In this way independence and obedience to the law will be reconciled.

Each citizen desires that the power he supports grant him through law the maximum number of advantages possible, even at the cost of oppressing other citizens. But this power has to reckon with the other power, which bears the demands of the other party. What then is the law going to be? It is going to be the compromise, explicit or implicit, between the two powers and the two parties. It is going to implement the maximization of advantage for both sides, with each obtaining less than it wanted. This form of liberty, in the sense of independence, facilitates the maximization of advantage for everybody. Take an example unknown to Montesquieu: imagine a society in which a powerful group wants education to be dispensed under the Church's direction, and another group of about equal strength wants it completely removed from the Church's influence. If this society has a representative regime of divided powers, neither of the two groups will be able to impose the law it wants. The only compromise possible will be that each group have the liberty to obtain the type of education it desires: one part of the educational establishment will be dependent on the Church, the other will be completely independent.

In such a system, the law tends to forbid any individual from imposing his will on another. But by that very fact, it forbids anyone else from imposing his will on him. By preventing the individual from imposing his will on another, it limits his independence; but by guaranteeing him the right to do what he wants, so long as that act does not involve exercising power over another, it protects his independence. The law has power only for preventing the excesses of one citizen's power over another. Thus, "asserting his independence whenever he pleases" and having "the right to do whatever the laws permit" become, in a free regime such as Montesquieu conceived of it, progressively synonymous.

Citizens who no longer exercise power over each other tend to distance themselves from one another, to live separately. In the same chapter, Montesquieu writes that "men, in this nation, would be more like confederates than fellow citizens." Astonishingly, he compares the relationships between citizens of a free regime with those linking independent and allied political bodies. One cannot suggest more clearly that these citizens live in a kind of state of nature, but one freed from fear. The free society founded on the separation of powers is a perfected state of nature: the citizens enjoy the advantages of the state of nature (they "act as they please") without suffering from its inconveniences (they are freed from war and fear).

What is important in the doctrine of the separation of powers is less the static definition of particular competences than the dynamic description of the relationship between civil society and two equally but differently representative powers, each acting as intermediary for parties. This interplay between society and divided power will always unfold according to the schema proposed by Montesquieu, even at a time when the separation between the executive and the legislative will no longer be anything but a memory. (Today, for example, confusion between them prevails in the form of "cabinet government," a form in which the head of government—the executive—is at the same time head of the parliamentary majority—the legislative.) The two powers are then no longer the executive and the legislative, but the "majority" and the "opposition." It is not that the opposition constitutionally shares power with the majority; on this point there is a considerable difference between the free regime described by

Montesquieu and contemporary democracies. But the very presence of the opposition, and the threat of its winning the next elections, are enough, as a general rule, to persuade the majority party to make moderate use of its power.

The motivating spirit of Montesquieu's liberal system is to separate the will from what it desires, or to prevent each person from doing what he cannot prevent himself from desiring. The people cannot do what they want, they can only elect representatives in the hope that they will do what the electorate wants; the representatives in turn cannot do what they themselves want, but must be keenly aware of what the executive wants; and the executive cannot do what it wants since it must seriously take into account what the legislature wants. A mechanism of decision making that makes sovereignty useless now replaces the absolute sovereignty of Hobbe's Leviathan and also that of Locke's legislative body. This mechanism is extremely different from deliberation as it was instituted in the Greek republics and described by Aristotle in book 4 of the *Politics*. Precisely because deliberation is a reasonable activity, the deliberating part of the city-state had to consider the need for compromise and moderation in the decisions it made. The point of compromise was fixed by the deliberation itself, according to its chosen ends, and the circumstances imposed on it. In ceding to the necessity of compromise, deliberation did not cease to be sovereign. The situation is entirely different in Montesquieu's liberal system. Far from being chosen by the sovereignty of deliberation, compromise is itself the sovereign of the decision, since what is decided is the result of the combined desires of the two powers.

We have now seen how, even if opinions differ greatly, it is nevertheless possible to reach an agreement. It is very difficult to reach it positively, very much easier to do it negatively. If we cannot achieve both what I want and what you want, why not try to achieve what neither of us wants? The two powers say to each other: I do not want you to govern, you do not want me to govern. Why not make the citizens independent of both our powers, why not liberate them, and the desired result will be achieved? The representation of society by a divided power results in the citizens being less governed, that is freer in Montesquieu's sense of the word liberty. Freedom is less doing what I want than being able not to do what you want me to do. It is doing what I want so long as I do not constrain you.

Fully constituted liberalism, which is fully constituted doctrinally only with Montesquieu, is based on two ideas: the idea of representation and the idea of separation of powers. The idea of representation postulates that the only legitimate power is founded on the consent of those subject to power. In such a regime, all powers within civil society born from the spontaneous interplay of economic and social life or from traditions come to seem essentially illegitimate since they are not representative. Hence they are slowly but surely eroded. All legitimate power is concentrated at the summit, in the political institution, in the state which alone represents members of society. The modern idea of representation leads naturally to a continuous increase of the state's power over society, because it continuously erodes the intrasocial powers that ensure the independence and solidity of this society. This is the paradox of representation: representative power tends necessarily to dominate the civil society that it claims to represent. In this sense, those who deplore society's growing dependence on the state are right.

But, simultaneously, because this representative state is divided between majority and opposition, its acts tend no less necessarily to be generally favorable to individual liberty. As I have tried to show, the compromise between the two powers is reached much more easily in the negative mode than in the positive: each power tends to exercise its power by preventing the other from obtaining what it wants. Thus what are sometimes called the citizen's "realms of freedom" inevitably grow. In this sense, those who celebrate the progress of individual liberty, the growing emancipation of individuals, are right.

Hence there is an essential ambivalence in the internal movements of democratic societies. It leads some people to describe them as totalitarianisms in disguise; others, as the most satisfying societies in human history, where each free and sovereign person uses the talents and satisfies the tastes nature has granted him. Both groups are both wrong and right. The reason is that today we are governed more exclusively by a state that governs us less. Insofar as we are less governed, we are, in a way, living more in a state of nature. And because this state of nature is still not a state of war, but offers us acceptable security and prosperity, we have no motive for leaving this state. We have thus fulfilled the original program of liberalism by reversing the order of the factors. The representative regime initially was the ingenious device making it possible to leave a state of nature that was essentially (Hobbes) if not even necessarily (Locke) unbearable; it became the ingenious device making it possible to live in an essentially satisfying state of nature. This diagnosis can hardly be contested even by those who denounce the benign "totalitarianism" of liberal societies. What makes them indignant about our societies is precisely this state of satisfaction: the quarrels and rebellions, the audacities and subversions, are all absorbed and recuperated by the system, to our general satisfaction.

A slight doubt can still, however, undermine this satisfaction. After all, an artificial or instituted state of nature that is still political is a contradiction in terms. Montesquieu himself discreetly suggested the difficulty when he said of the English that they were "confederates rather than fellow citizens." This alternative can and will be formulated as questions. Is each person primarily an independent member of "civil society" or a subject of the "state," a bourgeois or a citizen, a *homo oeconomicus* or a *homo politicus?* Does he belong first to the transnational or worldwide space of the "market" or rather to the territory of the "nation"? He belongs to both, it will be answered. But such an answer signifies that in spite of the reconciliation between the state of nature and the civil state by means of a free regime, we remain radically *divided:* the dividing line between the natural man and the citizen is now within us. To describe this division, to denounce the misfortune and corruption that it brings about, to seek to overcome it, will be the task of Montesquieu's—and liberalism's—most profound critic, Jean-Jacques Rousseau.

CHAPTER VI

Rousseau, Critic of Liberalism

IT SEEMS ANACHRONISTIC to present Rousseau as a critic of liberalism. After all, the first target of his indignation was the social and political order of the France he knew, which cannot be called liberal; the second was "society" as such, regardless of its political regime. But the fact that Rousseau criticized the ancient régime like everyone else in the second half of the eighteenth century must not lead us astray. In his eyes, the verdict was already in: the absolute monarchy was odious, and was already dead inside. If he crossed swords several times with "absolutism" or despotism, it was without particular anger. Besides, like Montesquieu before him, he was sure that a revolution would soon bring it down. What mattered to him was what was going to replace the monarchy, something that was already present in France and had already substantially transformed it. France was no longer characterized by the king's absolute power; it was ruled by *opinion*. Whose opinion? *Society's*. And what is *society*? It is inequality.

For Rousseau the king's favor no longer determined men's credit and thus their position. It was opinion, an authority with no specific organ and no specific place apart from "Paris," which had replaced Versailles. The credit that opinion conferred was attributed by no one in particular, but it was recognized and obeyed by all. This credit of opinion was directly related to credit in the financial sense of the term: one lent only to the wealthy, and those who had credit, for whatever reason, became wealthy.[1] Consequently, men were ranked not on the basis of their power, birth, competence, or even riches, but rather on the basis of this imperceptible credit of which wealth was only the outward or measurable sign. The society Rousseau was contemplating was not characterized by powers attributable to persons or institutions, but by an inequality relating only to itself, with no content or meaning other than itself. Men looked at each other "from above" or "from below" according to a point of view which had been that of power, but which power had deserted. The relationships of power had become simply that, "relationships." They were relationships of inequality. Therefore, the spirit of society was inequality.

This is where liberalism comes in. To repeat, the foundation of liberalism is the distinction between civil society and the state: the latter is the representative instrument of the former. Civil society tends to be self-sufficient. Within it, members are governed neither by political power nor by other members; each of them is the source of his actions. They freely exercise their talents to ensure their preservation and even the most comfortable preservation possible—they seek to "better their condition." They also want to gain recognition for their merits, in particular intellectual and artistic merits, from their equals. As for the state, by representing and serving the individuals' instinct for self-preservation it promulgates laws that guarantee to each person security and free pursuit of happiness as he conceives of it. These are the principles. But how do they function *in fact?*

In such a system, the individual is, hypothetically, the unique source of his actions. He obeys only himself. But what are the motives or ends of these actions, which are supposedly his own? He necessarily enters into relations with other individuals for his education, business, and pleasures. He depends on them without ruling them or being ruled by them. How are these individuals, in principle independent but in fact dependent, going to relate to each other? The answer is contained in the question: they are going to *compare* themselves to each other.

Comparing oneself to others is the misfortune and original sin of men in our societies. The misfortune is that the man who compares himself with others is always unhappy. There will always be someone richer than me, and even if I am the richest, I will not be the most handsome or most intelligent. The sin is that the man who compares himself is always corrupted or on the point of being so. Not only does the desire to be first lead him to commit the everyday mischief that the moral code condemns, it also obliges him to give others a pleasing image of himself, to flatter himself and flatter them. His exterior will never be in harmony with his interior and his life will be a permanent lie. Moreover, comparing oneself with others is paradoxical. For the man who lives by comparison is the one who, in his relationships with others, thinks only of himself, and in his relations with himself, thinks only of others.[2] He is the *divided* man.

In such a society based on universal comparison of all with all, it is natural that society place importance on the outcome of the comparison. The terms of the comparison being varied—power, birth, wealth, talents—this permits the comparison of comparisons, so to speak. And the inequality that sums up all the others, into which all the others can be converted, is that of money. Hence the importance of denouncing the rich more than the powerful in Rousseau's work. But for him, the rich man is not an economic category: he epitomizes a society founded on comparison, that is, on inequality among men who no longer *govern* themselves.

In Rousseau's eyes, this inequality, and the behavior of which it is both cause and effect, are not only to be found in the French society of his time. He simply happens to live in that society, and therefore know it best; it may be also that inequality and its consequences are more visible in that society. But fundamentally, the behavior was that of *modern* man in *modern* society: it was the same in Paris and London, Edinburgh and Naples. Modern man had become a *bourgeois;* he had ceased to be a *citizen.* The contrast between the bourgeois and the citizen, and the denunciation of the bourgeois as a degraded human type, are first found and best expressed in Rousseau's work. Consequently, the difference between the English liberal regime and the French absolutist regime was secondary. Rousseau had some kind words for English liberty, he also had some cruel ones. What mattered was that the motivating spirit of social life was identical in the two nations. The same human type tended to prevail: the bourgeois, the man who by withdrawing into himself distinguished his own good from the common good. But to find his own good, he needed others, on whom he was dependent while seeking to exploit them.

Yet, between France and England there was an incontestable difference. Hobbes and Locke formulated the principles of liberal or bourgeois individualism; the English founded the political regime destined to be inhabited by the bourgeois, who found it eminently suitable. But to carry out this *political* task, the bourgeois had to become citizens, at least for a certain period; by Rousseau's time this was undoubtedly over. The English had temporarily imposed on themselves the burdens of citizens so as subsequently to become bourgeois. Hence a certain equivocation in their political and social character, and Rousseau's apparent hesitation to make a political judgment concerning them. The French on the contrary became quite plainly bourgeois under the oppressive aegis of the absolute monarchy, which successfully prevented them from becoming citizens. (The English had for a time been citizens, though in a confused way in the sixteenth and the beginning of the seventeenth century.) It was thus in the French absolute monarchy that the psychology of modern bourgeois man developed and revealed itself most completely, while the English kept several traits of civic virility. For Rousseau, the very different place of women in the two societies attested to this fact.

What Rousseau leads us to see by his very revolt is the homogeneity of European history, the homogeneity of what he calls the "modern peoples." The author who best summarizes European history is Hobbes; he decisively substituted the bourgeois for the citizen and thus became Rousseau's principal modern interlocutor, in approval as in criticism. The French body politic developed continuously, without rupture, according to Hobbes's prescription. But the English body politic modified that prescription according to Locke's corrections. Absolutism thus produced the bourgeois which liberalism only imagined.

The time has come to listen to Rousseau's own voice. Here is how, from a genealogy of the goods and evils of society in general, he characterizes the bourgeois man of modern society.

> If this were the place to go into details, I would easily explain how, *even without the involvement of government,* inequality of *credit* and authority becomes inevitable between *individuals* as soon as, united in the same society, they are forced to *make comparisons* between themselves and to take into account differences they find in the continual use they have to make of one another. These differences are of several kinds; but in general wealth, nobility, or rank, power, and personal merit being the principal distinctions by which one is measured in society, I would prove that the agreement or conflict or these various forces is the surest indication of a well- or ill-constituted state. I would show that of these four types of inequality, as personal qualities are the origin of all the others, *wealth is the last to which they are reduced in the end* because, being the most immediately *useful to well-being* and the easiest to communicate, it is easily used to buy all the rest. . . . I would point out how much that universal desire for reputation, honors, and preferences, which devours us all, trains and compares talents and strengths; how much it stimulates and multiplies passions; and making all men *competitors, rivals,* or rather *enemies,* how many reverses, successes, and catastrophes of all kinds it causes daily by making so many contenders race the same course.[3]

I have pointed out that Rousseau's principal modern interlocutor was Hobbes. We must take a brief look at their relationship. They have one fundamental point in common: all the political misfortunes of European peoples come from Christianity, more precisely from the constitution of a Christian religious power distinct from and in rivalry with the political power: "This double power," says Rousseau, "has resulted in a perpetual conflict of jurisdiction that has made any good polity impossible in Christian states." He continues: "Of all Christian authors, the philosopher Hobbes is the only one who correctly saw the evil and the remedy, who dared to propose the reunification of the two heads of the eagle, and the complete return to political unity, without which no state or government will ever be well constituted."[4] But their agreement ends here, because the political unity constructed by Hobbes is despotic and Rousseau adds immediately afterwards that it is "horrible and false."

Rousseau thinks that it is possible to assure political and social unity without despotism, a possibility that was revealed by the ancient city-state (Sparta in particular) and by republican Rome. In these city-states, free from despotism, real citizens were closely united in a common interest, that of the city-state. It is by comparison with such citizens, with Plutarch's heroes, that the modern bourgeois reveals his contemptible character. In his patriotism, the ancient citizen's own interest merged with that of the city-state. He was not divided, he was whole; and because he was whole, he was both happy and virtuous.

Hobbes sees in the prestige of the ancient city-states the second major motive, after the Church's claims, for the disorders that led to the English Civil War; the prestige of the idea of civic liberty stirs up the spirit of disobedience, and the spirit of disobedience causes civil war (see chapter 3). In his eyes, civil peace has two great enemies: the enthusiastic reader of the Bible, who believes that he feels the infusion of God's grace in his soul, and the enthusiastic reader of Plutarch who believes that he feels the beating heart of a new Epaminondas in his chest. Rousseau readily admits that ancient liberty and civic virtue made little of the individual's desire for self-preservation. What mattered to the citizen was the preservation and glory of his city-state, not his individual preservation; and for his own glory, what could be more glorious than dying for the homeland? In some of his most eloquent passages, Rousseau calls into question the modern and bourgeois Hobbesian ideal of peace: "Long ago, Greece flourished in the midst of the cruelest wars. Blood flowed freely, and the whole country was covered with men. . . . A little agitation gives vitality to souls, and it is not so much peace as freedom that makes the species truly prosper."[5]

What Rousseau especially criticizes in Hobbes's doctrine is not the state-controlled "superstructure"; of course, he criticizes it, too, for absolutism, and on this point he agrees with the liberals. It is rather the individualistic civil "infrastructure" that he criticizes, and which is the basis of all modern politics, absolutist as well as liberal. For him, the condition of the modern individual is contradictory: too independent, given his dependency on others, he is also too dependent. Modern man is forced to collaborate with others yet he is thinking only of himself. The division between the political and religious powers that Hobbes overcomes at the level of state control, and at the price of despotism, is found again in civil society. The division between the Christian and the citizen becomes the division between the individual man and the member of society, social man. The conflict between the Christian and the citizen becomes the conflict between the individual and society.

It is now possible to characterize the three fundamental positions that define respectively absolutism, liberalism, and Rousseau's thought. Absolutism and liberalism have the same central element: the individual. For the former, individuals can be held together only by a power that is external to and sovereign over them, because of their proud and rebellious nature. For liberalism, on the other hand, individuals are much less naturally rebellious than absolutism thinks, and spontaneously form peaceful relationships, giving rise to a society which, it not entirely self-sufficient, at least needs no absolute government to hold it together. The foundation of this confidence lies in the conviction that each person's pursuit of his personal interest leads to the promotion of the public interest. The specific arena for this harmony between the personal and public interests is economic life. The pursuit of his private interest leads each producer to increase the productivity of his work; in turn, this increase raises the quantity of values available in society, so that the poor in an acquisitive society live more comfortably than the wealthy in a society where the acquisitive instinct is undeveloped. The agricultural laborer, according to Locke's example, is better off than an Indian king in America. Added to the direct economic effect of the emancipation of the individual's acquisitiveness are the no less important indirect moral effects. One of the major themes of Montesquieu's *The Spirit of the Laws* is that the development of commerce leads to a relaxing of mores, in a twofold sense. On the one hand, by multiplying their relationships through commerce, the members of different civil societies get to know each other and thus progressively lose their prejudices that nourish aggressiveness and so often lead to war; on the other hand, once commercial life has definitely gathered speed, brutal interventions in society by political power become detrimental for the power itself.[6] According to Montesquieu, the expansion of commerce in Europe was obliging the princes and states "to be cured of Machiavellism."[7] Developments in the sciences, arts, and commerce matched the progress in peace, security, and freedom: this is the liberal diagnosis of the evolution of the modern world, this is the foundation of its optimism or progressivism. It is against this optimism or progressivism that Rousseau directs his cutting criticism.

Rousseau asks: what happens to the *soul* of someone who lives according to the maxims of such a society? Everybody is obliged to live by them, since all the citizens are dependent and competitors. Since they are dependent, they are obliged to do no harm to each other. As competitors, they are obliged not to do good, or at least not to want to do good to each other. None of the great human passions can emerge in such a society. Instead of the active love of fellow citizens and active hate of enemies, which unfurl simultaneously in the soul of the ancient citizen and give him his vigor and grandeur, we find that self-love (*amour-propre*) is the unique passion of modern man. Self-love is not genuine love for oneself (*amour de soi*), it is even contrary to it in a way. Self-love lives by comparison; it is the desire to be esteemed by others as highly as one esteems oneself. It is condemned to be thwarted because everyone has the same self-love and experiences the same desire. Self-love knows that it cannot be satisfied, and it hates others for their own self-love. It nourishes in the soul the miserable taste for oneself and impotent hatred for others. In such a society, man lives only for the gaze of others, whom he hates.

It is very important to note that this description of the principle of modern social life in no way contradicts the brief sketch of English life drawn by Montesquieu. "All the passions being unrestrained, hatred, envy, jealousy, and an ambitious desire of riches and honors, appear in their extent; were it otherwise, the state would be in the condition of a man weakened by sickness, who is without passions because he is without strength."[8] As can be seen, Montesquieu even admits that these moral phenomena are not superficial or accidental, but that they constitute the basis of English life. Here then are two great philosophers, almost contemporaries, who describe the principle of modern life very similarly. But one does it very briefly and soberly (it is the price to pay for liberty), while the other deploys a dazzling subtlety and bewitching eloquence to denounce self-love in all its aspects, in all its ramifications and consequences. How can one speak of liberty, Rousseau asks, when no individual will can get what it wants, when those who seem to command are in fact slaves to opinion—when, in a word, the freedom of all is only the impotence of all? What Montesquieu considers as a long-sought political system capable of protecting human nature, Rousseau sees as the institutionalization of human debasement.

It would be highly presumptuous of anyone to decide hastily between Montesquieu and Rousseau. Rousseau's strength lies in the extraordinary persuasiveness of his description of modern man, to which we owe some of the most powerful achievements of modern literature. Montesquieu's strength is less dazzling, but no less convincing in the end: he proves that there is no desirable substitute for liberalism. Absolutism, of which the French monarchy represented the perfected example, could no longer be a real possibility. Its very success led to its downfall: precisely because he was elevated so high above the society he ruled, the king had been in a position to break up to a considerable extent the power of the various intermediary social bodies—seigniories, parliaments, Church—that constituted and also divided society. He had been in a position to create in their place a unified society composed of individuals, each one obeying the king directly, independently of the intermediary social bodies. The king had thus given society the possibility of perceiving itself as a unity, even, or especially, without him. The medium of this new unity was opinion. Besides, one can deduce the necessary abolition of absolutism from the very principles on which Hobbes founded it. Leviathan's raison d'être was to pacify relations among members of society. As that task was ever more efficiently accomplished, Leviathan became superfluous.

Once absolutism self-destructs in this way, what political forms can be counted as viable? The idea of empire having been absorbed by absolute monarchy, there remains the city-state. Each time that a political order in Europe approaches its end and the question of succession arises, the idea of the ancient city-state reemerges with its prestige intact. That was the case during the Renaissance, as we saw earlier; at that time, monarchy prevailed because it was better equipped to confront the theologico-political problem. That was the case again in the eighteenth century when the exhaustion of the monarchical form became ever more noticeable. Montesquieu took this possibility seriously, yet rejected it resolutely. In his eyes, the Greek city-states and Rome were great achievements, superior in many respects to modern monarchies. But their advantages were bought at a very great cost: they were essentially warlike political bodies, in which the individual was certainly not oppressed as he is by despotism, but in which he was subjected to an exhausting social discipline.[9] Modern man, whom commerce has led to acquire new habits, would find it very difficult to bear such inhuman constraints; and it would be absurd for him to take on such a burden. The English found a radically new means of escaping any risk of despotism, one that was also more satisfying since it transformed the individual from warrior into a proprietor of goods or talents, engaged in "making good use of his independence whenever he pleases."

As for Rousseau, what substitute for liberalism does he propose? In his case, there is a great temptation to answer, the ancient city-state. And it is true, as I have noted, that ancient greatness is the criterion that in his eyes establishes modern degradation. But does he really propose the ancient city-state, or some new political system similar to it, as an effective and desirable possibility? The answer is no. The reason is twofold. First, such a revival is impossible. Monarchies built large states, whereas ancient public-spiritedness required a body politic of reduced dimensions. And there is a second, deeper reason: even if the ancient city-state were still possible, it would not be desirable. In Rousseau's own eyes, the ancient city-state is not really a credible model.

A quotation taken from the *Social Contract* will make the ambiguity of Rousseau's position clear:

> What! Freedom can only be maintained with the support of servitude? Perhaps. The two extremes meet. Everything that is not in nature has its problems, and civil society more than all the rest. There are some unfortunate situations when one cannot preserve one's freedom except at the expense of others, and when the citizen can only be perfectly free if the slave is completely enslaved. Such was Sparta's situation. As for you, modern peoples, you have no slaves, but you are slaves. You pay for their freedom with your own. You boast of that preference in vain; I find it more cowardly than humane.
>
> I do not mean by all this that it is necessary to have slaves, nor that the right of slavery is legitimate, since I have proved the opposite.[10]

The Greek city-state is the principle of indictment of modern liberal society, but it does not furnish a substitute for liberalism.[11]

What then are Rousseau's positive principles? This a is particularly delicate question. For him, modern society makes men nasty and unhappy; but it is unnatural for man to be nasty and unhappy. Therefore, this society is unnatural. The good society can only be one that conforms to man's nature. Thus the true nature of man has to be discovered: this is Rousseau's great investigation.

Precisely because our society is unnatural, because the man we see is not natural man, the investigation is particularly difficult and perhaps impossible. Can we at least find a guide among the authors who have sought the truth about the state of nature? The greatest of such moderns is Hobbes. But it is quite obvious that his "state of nature," in which everyone is bent on seeking ever more power and getting the upper hand, is simply a reflection of our social state. Our social state, one might retort, is peaceful, whereas the state of nature fosters the war of all against all. But the difference is superficial, since our passions in time of peace are the very same as in the state of war. And the very fact that they do not dare approach a state of war, that they are condemned to inactivity, only makes them more corrupting. What Hobbes exposes is the very depths of the heart of civilized man.

So then what is the solution? There is only one: to remove one by one the veils that human convention and artifice have draped over the true face of man, to isolate the simplest operations of the human soul, to be able to say at last: "Here is man, man in his true nature!" This is the approach taken by Rousseau in his *First Discourse*, the "Discourse on the Origin of Inequality."

Since any society implies conventions and artifice, one has to consider man prior to conventions, artifice, or society: the original solitary individual. And since man develops his faculties only through the development of society, this original solitary individual will not be a man, but rather a kind of animal endowed with *perfectibility*, that is with the capacity to become a man. I have tried to suggest why Rousseau engages in this strange quest for natural man: the revulsion evoked by perhaps the most sociable, pleasant, and artificial society that Europe had even known naturally thrust him toward the opposite extreme. But there is another reason, one more intellectual and political. We have seen how Hobbes, in order to confront the theologico-political problem, posited a hypothetical individual who precedes what I have called the two obediences—the obedience to human law and to divine law. Through him Hobbes reconstructs the legitimate state finally delivered from conflict between the civil and religious powers. But since the entity being sought is imaginary, nothing can end this investigation, for there are always good reasons for going further than one's predecessors. Or rather, this search reaches a necessary end only when the original man ceases to be a man. This is the point reached by Rousseau.

The political consequences of this new and ultimate definition of the natural "man" are considerable. At this stage natural man no longer has anything social or specifically human about him: the natural "man" is one who lives outside of or beyond any society. Not just our society, but every society, even the best, is contrary to man's nature. What then is the meaning of political protest, of the search for a society conforming to man's nature, if man is not by nature social—if society as such is contrary to his nature? This is Rousseau's problem. Rousseau's thought incarnates that paradoxical moment when man's nature is most vehemently appealed to in the political debate, and when it ceases in fact to serve as its regulator and criterion. This theoretical contradiction opens new possibilities for political action. On the one hand, the idea of human nature oppressed by an unjust social order gives an eminent dignity to any social or political discontent; on the other, the fact that this human nature can no longer be defined positively opens an immense opportunity, an unlimited space for action destined to right all social wrongs. It is the point when revolution, in the modern sense of the term, becomes possible.

It will probably be objected that I make Rousseau more confused than he was. After all, his *Social Contract* is a quite precise analysis of the conditions of a legitimate political regime. Thus he himself proposed a positive substitute for liberalism. But what is the motivating spirit of the *Social Contract?* We have already seen that society is corrupt and man is unhappy when the individual is divided; man in nature is happy and good because he is *whole,* because he is self-sufficient. The good polity ought to preserve this individual unity, integrity, and self-sufficiency. It is obviously impossible to do that. What might be done, however, is to succeed in identifying each individual with the polity itself: in that way, no member of the body politic will any longer distinguish his own being from the common being. He will be *whole* because he will become one with the body politic. According to a phrase that is not found in the *Social Contract* but that summarizes its project admirably: everyone will have for a state so constructed "that delicate sentiment that any isolated man feels only for himself."[12] The *general will* thus becomes the principle and locus of identification of all particular wills. It gives existence as well as legitimacy to the new artificial individual with whom all natural individuals identify. All Rousseau's analyses concerning rights and wills have a single end: to show how this unity, this identity can be established.

Such a state can be said to conform to man's nature only insofar as it is *whole,* just as the natural individual is *whole.* But it can also be called artificial, and even unnatural, since it must "be capable of changing human nature, so to speak; of transforming each individual, who by himself is a perfect and solitary whole, into a part of a larger whole from which this individual receives, in a sense, his life and his being; of altering man's constitution in order to strengthen it."[13] Thus, the principal difficulty in the doctrine of the *Social Contract* lies in the contradiction between the state's nature and its origin. According to its nature, as we have just seen, the state realizes the identity between the individual and the social body, the identity between the individual's instinct for preservation and that of the social body. Now, the origin of the state lies in the instinct for *individual* preservation. On this matter, Rousseau's point of view closely resembles Locke's. Rousseau remarks that at a certain stage in the state of nature, individuals are no longer capable of protecting their lives and goods all alone; thus they join forces, under the sovereign direction of a general will, to protect their lives and goods. The goods, transformed from the precarious possessions that they were, now become true property, guaranteed by authorities responsible for public order. The social contract is a contract of *proprietors*. But at that very instant, Rousseau specifies, the aforementioned proprietor, until then engaged only in self-preservation, literally changes nature and his own self comes to identify with the common self of the new public person. This individual who was as solidly proprietor, as completely bourgeois as the Lockean man, becomes more rigorously *citizen* than the most hardened Spartan. All the contradictions that the reader finds in the *Social Contract* have their source in this change.

Consequently, the *Social Contract* cannot possibly contain a political program. On the one hand, it covers and repeats Locke's teaching and can be placed under the liberal heading; on the other, it opens up a radically indeterminate future, in which the only guide will be the idea of social unity, of the identification of each individual's interest and will with those of all. The only way to be certain that this will is realized, that the public interest does not merge with any particular interest, is to place the public interest in contradiction with *all* private interests and to measure the realization of the public interest by the contradiction it poses to all private interests. The unity of all will be made perceptible by the oppression of all. In this sense, it is not absurd that Robespierre thought he had fulfilled Rousseau's idea. Must it be said then that Rousseau's thought is both liberal and Robespierrist? In fact, it can seem to be one and the other only because it is neither. To see this we must look more closely at his interpretation of property.

I have said that in the *Social Contract* Rousseau repeats the Lockean genesis of the body politic. But Rousseau in no way shares Locke's idea of property. To understand Rousseau's thought on this point, we have to turn to the *Second Discourse,* which he considers his "most philosophical" work. In it, Rousseau argues that the Lockean conception of the right to property is superficial. Certainly he agrees with the English philosopher that labor is at the origin of the *idea* of property; but labor cannot be at the origin of the *right* to property. The gist of the debate is this: Locke asserts that the original legitimate appropriation takes place on the basis of content, that those who appropriate the fruits of the earth by their labor are the "industrious," who rightfully ignore those who are mere "quarrelers."

Rousseau denies this and replies that the act of appropriation through work is nothing but *force*. By what right have you closed this common pasture where my cow is grazing? You say you are working and producing, but what does that matter to me? I have asked nothing of you. In Locke's definition, labor is above all the silent, solitary relationship of the individual with nature; rights, by their very definition, actually or tacitly presuppose a relationship among men, the exchange of words. Labor cannot establish the right to property.

In the stage immediately prior to the political institution, Rousseau tells us, the state of nature is revealed as "the most horrible state of war," marked by a conflict among the "right" to work, the "right" of the strongest, the "right" of need, the "right" of the first occupant, and so on. To resolve this conflict, the language of law must be instituted; people must *speak*. Who is going to speak? Those who relatively suffer most from this state, who are, paradoxically, the rich. Since, for the rich, the instinct for preservation extends beyond their own bodies to their goods, their instinct is bound to be more developed than that of the poor, who have only their bodies and their lives. Consequently, the rich are going to take the initiative in speaking the word that founds the body politic. They are going to conceive of "the most well-thought-out plan that has ever entered the human mind," they are going to propose to everyone, and in particular to the poor, the constitution of a body politic that will protect everyone's goods (above all those of the rich) by using everyone's force (above all that of the poor). Inequality is thus established and human misfortune assured.

Property exposes and condenses the contradiction of the human world. This contradiction is born from labor and the inequality of properties because it was originally founded on the difference in capacities for work, that is, on an inequality of strength. At the same time, the one who is strongest or richest is also the one who is weakest because he is the most dependent: his being is more extensive, since it incorporates his goods. The political institution aims at compensating for this original weakness of the rich by bringing them the strength that naturally they always need, which is in fact the strength of the poor. The law is the sole means by which the strength of the poor can be put to lasting use.[14]

Hence the extraordinary oscillation of Rousseau's judgment on property. On the one hand, he defines it as "sacred," even more sacred than freedom, because "more difficult to defend": possessions are weaker than the individual possessing them because they have no hands to defend themselves. On the other, he sees in it the original usurpation, the proof that the ultimate foundation of every civil society lies in an act of force that can never become fully just, in conformity with rights. Consequently, laws, even the best ones, have a contradictory finality: they must aim to correct the original inequality of properties which has no foundation other than force, but they also must condone this inequality, since these laws bring force to the "unequal" property that most needs it. The main purpose of political law, and thus of the political institution, is to correct *and* condone the inequality of properties. As Rousseau says in *Emile:* "This disadvantage is inevitable, and without exception."

The ultimate paradox of Rousseau's thought could be formulated in this way. On the one hand, society is essentially contrary to nature; on the other, it comes near to conforming to nature only insofar as it imposes the greatest unity possible on its members, identifying each person with everyone and the whole—in short, only insofar as it changes man's nature. Because society is contrary to man's nature, it is in being most contrary to him that it conforms most closely to him.

Such an expression is of course "contradictory." But it ceases to be so if we add that it is in man's nature to be contradictory, that this expression only reflects man's inner contradictions: it is natural for man to change his nature because man, at bottom, is not nature but *liberty*. And liberty is that power by which man gives orders to his own nature, or changes his nature, or is a law unto himself. The striking "contradiction" of Rousseau's political doctrine indicates and requires the implementation of a new definition of man: man's nature is not to have a nature, but to be free. By this very fact, Rousseau's antiliberal thought is going to provide content to the hypothetical being on which liberalism constructed itself, the individual. Liberalism reached its principle, the individual, only indirectly, by the roundabout means of the state of nature. It can even be said that the individual reached in this way was hardly "free" since his behavior was, so to speak, mechanically determined by the necessity to flee from evil, to preserve his life. With Rousseau, freedom becomes immediate to the individual, it is a feeling, both experienced and required, of *autonomy*. Liberalism's individual was not inwardly free; Rousseau is not a liberal but his individual is free. Thus he is going to provide liberal societies with the inmost and immediate feeling by which the individual becomes aware of himself, by which man feels himself to be, or tries to be, an individual.

At the same time, this inmost and immediate feeling of freedom, an essential ingredient of liberal societies, is also a danger for them. If man is liberty, autonomy, if he is the being who makes his own laws, he cannot derive his motives from nature without demeaning himself. Faced with the new definition of liberty, the old liberal liberty based on the natural necessity of self-preservation appears pathetic, weak, and vulgar. Determined by nature, liberal liberty is already no longer liberty. And since liberty, whether ancient or new, cannot act without a motive, the new liberty is going to seek a motive commensurate with its own sublimity. The Revolution will be the act by which liberty supplies its own motive, by which man raises himself above the dictates of his nature.

   With Rousseau, modern political thought reaches its ultimate expression and perplexity. It turns against liberalism only because it has carried through its original impetus and logic to the end: constructing an indivisible body politic from supposedly radically independent individuals. That means both that it fails to replace liberalism with another political doctrine founded on different principles, and that it holds over liberalism a vague and fearsome menace. This is the menace of a revolution responsible for imposing an imperious and unspecified unity on the dispersed individuals that liberalism supposedly does not sufficiently unite, of a revolution charged with actualizing the ineffable liberty that liberalism keeps in the dark. The French Revolution will follow in its very evolution the rhythm of Rousseau's thought. It will suddenly appear in 1789 with the aim of giving, at long last, adequate protection to the security and property of individuals; in 1793, it will turn against this security and property so as to obtain the absolute unity of the new body politic; on 9 Thermidor, it will abandon this "unnatural" effort which tended to nullify its own foundation, and will become reconciled with property and its inequality. But this reconciliation in turn, will remain essentially precarious. By raising itself above all the determinations of nature, the revolutionary act opened up an indeterminate "possibility" that no politics would henceforth be able either to forget or fulfill. This possibility, which is impossible, casts man's political nature into a new element, that of an elusive, uncontrollable, and sovereign *history*. And for controlling history, the Revolution bequeathed to Europe an extraordinarily active and powerful figure of political unity: the *nation*.

   To say that with Rousseau modern political thought reached its limits is to say that after him there was no longer any political philosophy in the strict or original sense.[15] As we have seen, once the idea of nature has been exhausted, the question of the best political regime conforming to man's nature can no longer be posed as such. Nature ceases to be the criterion, the reference, or the model. Two other criteria are going to take its place: history and liberty. All political considerations and theories after the French Revolution will develop within philosophies of history and will be subordinated to them.

   The liberal doctrine rested on the distinction between civil society and the state. Rousseau established that this distinction is possible only because both terms have their source and foundation in a third term incorporating both of them. He is the first to bring out in all its clarity the third term, which he christens with a name that will last: "society." Rousseau made modern man aware that he does not live essentially in a body politic or a state, or in an economic system, but above all in society. In his eyes, modern man lives primarily in the element of society inasfar as he adopts the point of view of *inequality* in his relations with his fellow men. This is not particular inequality, economic or political, but simply inequality at large, an abstract and therefore omnipresent determination of social life. In the same train of thought, Rousseau extracts the contrary idea, just as abstract and destined to become just as omnipresent, that of *equality*.

If, less than a century later, Tocqueville could describe modern democratic society as based on the idea of and passion for equality, it was not only because the French Revolution and Rousseau's "influence" did their job and the new society was actually "more equal" than the former one. It was also because the inequality observed by Rousseau contains or leads to the equality described by Tocqueville. More important than the inequality or the equality that characterize society is society itself, a vital and indiscernible element that nurtures men, and from which they seek to escape when they no longer command each other.

CHAPTER VII

Liberalism after
the French Revolution

I HAVE TRIED to show in the preceding chapters how the development and consolidation of the liberal point of view had their origin in the theologico-political problem, and more precisely in Hobbes's response to it. Rousseau put an end to this first cycle of liberalism by heightening to the breaking point the tensions that had given liberalism its original vigor and thrust. The second liberalism, which emerged in the first half of the nineteenth century, bore little resemblance to the first: it was separated from it by Rousseau and the French Revolution. The task of this liberalism was, in a way, to absorb the shock produced by this complex of events, feelings, and ideas.

We must begin by pointing out that the liberalism of the nineteenth century accepts and approves the French Revolution, not only its results but the act itself (if not all its acts). The point is worth stressing. Burke, who can also be called liberal, was nevertheless not followed by any of the great French liberals in his condemnation of the French Revolution.[1] Certainly, they made distinctions within the Revolution, condemning, for example, the terrorist phase. But fundamentally they were, intellectually and also emotionally, on the side of the revolutionaries and against the ancien régime. For us their attitude is surprising: in our retrospective viewpoint, "liberties" were rather better guaranteed, in fact if not in principle, under the ancien régime, at least in its final period, than during the Revolution or the Empire, as they themselves sometimes admit. How can their revolutionary enthusiasm, which seems not to be shared by French liberals today, be explained?

The most obvious explanation is reasonably convincing. After all, the ancien régime was founded, at least officially, on the very principles against which liberalism originally rose up: absolute sovereignty of the king and semipolitical power of the Church. On the other side, the revolutionaries and the members of the Constituent Assembly set themselves the task of carrying out the liberal program, of constructing a body politic based on representation and the separation of powers that would truly guarantee security, equality of rights, and property. But this cannot be the whole story. After all, the revolutionary experience had just established that the representative principle could turn into despotism, that the people's sovereignty could be confiscated by a handful of men; in short, the liberal conception of political order was fraught with mortal danger for liberties.

Where did the French Revolution take place, in what social setting, what political context, in what aspect of human association? It did not occur in civil society, whose life was suspended and organs destroyed; nor did it occur within the context of the state, since all the laws of political action and wisdom were found lacking. The revolutionaries were claiming to construct the state that would at last adequately represent society, but they belonged neither to state nor to society. They aimed beyond both of them and thereby invented a new role for man.

But this new role was implied, without being acknowledged, by the very distinction between civil society and the state on which liberalism had been working for a century and a half. Liberal man, capable of splitting himself into proprietor and citizen, could be neither one nor the other: he was implicitly a *third man,* different from both proprietor and citizen. The unfolding of the French Revolution made strikingly apparent a human situation and a human role that liberalism implied without revealing. I am not suggesting that the French Revolution was liberal as such or that the development of liberalism necessarily led to the Revolution. There is something else at stake, which requires us to examine public feeling in the postrevolutionary period.

After the Revolution, the men of the nineteenth century no longer lived merely in civil society or the state, they lived in a third element that received various names, usually "society" or "history." Regardless of what it was called, this element had the greatest authority. This "society" then was more than and different from "civil society": the latter had been created by the totality of relationships spontaneously formed by men, transformed by the desire for preservation, while the former had no explicit natural foundation. Its authority did not lie in nature, but in "history," in the historical evolution.

It is true that, from the seventeenth century on and especially in the eighteenth century, Europeans had felt that a process independent of political events was changing the state of social man, thanks to progress in the sciences, art, and commerce. But this process was perceived as a technical improvement of man's social nature. Man did not cease to live in nature, he simply was living better thanks to this improvement. That something entirely different was at stake in the nineteenth century is revealed by the most cursory comparison of the writings of Montesquieu and Benjamin Constant, two authors who have more in common than any other thinkers on the two sides of the French Revolution. There is no prerevolutionary author who grants more authority to history, understood as development of "knowledge" and "commerce," than Montesquieu. There is no pre-revolutionary author who asserts as much as he the decisive importance of historical development for human security and liberty. Unlike Constant, however, he did not have the feeling of *living* in the element of history, under the authority of history. Montesquieu wanted to establish history's authority but did not feel it. This difference is so important that it quite often blinds Constant to the fact that Montesquieu is saying the same thing as he.

It is definitely from the Revolution that this feeling dates. More precisely, it derives from the fact that the Revolution failed to develop adequate political institutions. The Revolution, therefore, could not be considered the foundation of a new body politic, still less a mere change in regime—the only two definitions of political "revolution" available until then. The Revolution offered the original spectacle of a political change of unheard-of scope, yet having no stable political effects, of a political upheaval impossible to settle, of an interminable and indeterminate event. The fact that men had the feeling of living in a third element, a "metapolitical" element, as it were, revealed by the Revolution, can be confirmed by the religious interpretation soon to be given to the notions of "society" and "history." Although the eighteenth century had been so hostile to religion, and the Revolution had conducted a violent dechristianization, the first part of the nineteenth century was in fact extraordinarily "religious." I do not mean to say that the French docilely reintegrated the Church into society, which did not happen; nevertheless, they began to interpret political and social events in religious terms, such that their political considerations became inseparable from the religious ones. The observation applies to everyone, or almost everyone, in the nineteenth century—to the liberals as well as the Saint-Simonians, to Chateaubriand as well as Quinet, to Tocqueville as well as Michelet. Here, however, I am considering only the liberal authors: this third element of which I am speaking, this metapolitics that determines politics, is actually Christianity "realizing" itself.

And indeed, if men feel themselves to be living in a third element, which is neither social nature nor political art, they cannot conceive of this element as real, other than by appealing to the only conceivable third term, one that is essentially different from nature and art, and stands above them—like religion. Simultaneously, since what is at stake here is not the soul's salvation but the understanding of society, these authors bent religion to fit the century, and made Christianity a "secular religion." For Chateaubriand as for Tocqueville, the new equality of civil and political rights is the last conquest of the Gospel, its fulfillment so long and so mysteriously deferred.

Because of our long experience, we have now become flexible. We move in this third element of "society" or "history" like fish in water, and even consider the notion of "culture" to be incontrovertible. Consequently, atheists as well as Christians today run the risk of being blind to the internal necessity of this variety of nineteenth century religion, which, too religious to be genuine politics, too political to be true religion, reveals the extreme precariousness of the "third man" whom we have become.

The second aspect of liberalism's relationship to the Revolution is that while accepting the revolutionary event's authority, and even adhering to the revolutionary religion, liberals will distinguish the Revolution's politics from its religion. They will endeavor to elaborate theoretically and practically the political institutions entailed by the Revolution, yet made unworkable by its religion. What defines the liberal project after the Revolution is its desire to secularize the secular religion to which it adheres; what characterizes the liberal after the Revolution is that he is an atheist under the true God, under the God in whom he believes. Hence liberals will also be critics, and sometimes very sharp ones, of the Revolution. In terms of practical politics, they will be followers of the Revolution rather than "reactionaries" demanding a "return" to the ancien régime; but they will also be critics who wish to "continue" or "deepen" the Revolution, and hence make impossible the stabilization of the liberal institutions implied by its principles.

CHAPTER VIII

Benjamin Constant and the Liberalism of Opposition

IT WAS UNDOUBTEDLY with Benjamin Constant that the liberal ambivalence toward the revolutionary event was most perceptible. On the one hand, he was unreservedly for the Revolution and against the ancien régime; he approved of not only its principles, but even certain of its less liberal measures. On the other hand, he was an extremely penetrating and severe critic of the "spirit" or "style" or "mores" of revolutionary, and later imperial, politics. This is how he conceived of the Revolution's meaning: "Regardless of the various banners under which people have embarked on and supported that struggle we have witnessed, and of which we have often been victims, it has always been fundamentally the struggle of the elective against the hereditary system. It is the principal question of the French Revolution, and so to speak, the question of the century."[1] Constant was also on the side of the elective system since it is founded on equality, which is the ultimate goal of human history: "The perfectibility of the human species is nothing other than the tendency toward equality. . . . Equality alone conforms to the truth, that is to the respective relationships of things and men to each other."[2]

Equality no longer has its place in the hypothetical state of nature imagined by the prerevolutionary liberals, a hypothesis Constant ridiculed. Its place is *history*, more precisely the completion of history, conceived of as the necessary progress of equality. One could also say that history appears as an incorporating notion, as the newly perceived element in which humanity transforms itself, because the different political, social, and religious forms can be considered together, described, and classified in terms of a growing equality. At the same time, however, Constant follows the works of the state of nature theorists even though he disdains them. If he considers that "equality alone conforms to truth," it is not because these theorists demonstrated that political legitimacy could be conceived of and produced only by starting from the hypothesis of equal individuals. Why then consider that the elective or representative regime is founded on the authority of history, an arena of human perfectibility, rather than on that of nature?

I suggested earlier a few of the reasons why liberal authors, and more generally postrevolutionary authors, had accepted this substitution of authority. In Constant's case, there was also a very specific political reason. The hypothesis of the state of nature leads necessarily, as we have seen, to founding the body politic on the idea of an absolute or supreme sovereignty. For Constant, the Revolution had just proved that there is no more dangerous idea for political liberties and even for simple social propriety. On the other hand, what is to be represented is no longer the individual's absolute right to self-preservation, but a complex group of previously constituted and incessantly changing interests, properties, and relationships. And if what is to be represented is what is brought about by the spontaneous movement of history in society, then the representative can no longer claim absolute sovereignty: he has to place himself in the service of social movement. Here the goal, or at least the result, of Constant's "historicism" is to limit decisively the legitimate field of political action. If history is the authority, if the "natural" arena of history's action is civil society, then political authority finds itself in an essentially subordinate position.

But, one might say, cannot history's authority also serve to justify despotism? What answer can be given to a government that declares that the historical stage reached by society requires X? What answer can be given to Danton when he declares, "These priests, this nobility are not guilty, but they have to die, because they are out of place, they hinder the movement of things and get in the way of the future"?[3] At that point, Constant rediscovers the criterion of nature: these are things that power has no right to do, regardless of the situation. Thus Constant's liberalism, like postrevolutionary liberalism generally, moves between two unequal authorities: first that of history, and then that of nature. But it is always in order to limit the jurisdiction of political power that one or the other authority is invoked. The fact remains that this uncertainty in the criterion of judgment introduces instability into Constant's analysis of the Revolution and the Empire. We must consider that analysis.

I have just said that the delicate question concerns the idea of sovereignty, in particular the sovereignty of the people such as the Revolution claimed to implement it, drawing inspiration from Rousseau. Constant completely accepts the principle of the sovereignty of the people, and also echoes Rousseau's language:

> Our present constitution formally recognizes the principle of the sovereignty of the people, that is the supremacy of the general will over any particular will. Indeed this principle cannot be contested. In our days many have attempted to obscure it; the evils which were caused and the crimes which were committed on the pretext of enforcing the general will lend apparent strength to the reasonings of those who would like to assign a different source to the authority

of governments. Nevertheless those reasonings cannot stand against the simple definition of the words which they use. The law must be either the expression of the will of all, or that of the will of some. What would be the origin of exclusive privilege if you should grant it to that small number? If it is power, then power belongs to whoever takes it. It does not constitute a right, and if you acknowledge it as legitimate, it will be equally legitimate whoever sets his hands on it, and everyone will want to conquer it in his turn. If you suppose that the power of a small number is sanctioned by the assent of all, then that power becomes the general will.[4]

Here Constant asserts the incontestable character of the sovereignty principle and recognizes the dangers of its application. He continues:

But while we recognize the rights of that will, that is the sovereignty of the people, it is necessary, indeed imperative, to understand its exact nature and to determine its precise extent.

Without a precise and exact definition, the triumph of the theory could become a calamity in its application. The abstract recognition of the sovereignty of the people does not in the least increase the amount of liberty given to individuals. If we attribute to that sovereignty an amplitude which it must not have, liberty may be lost notwithstanding that principle, or even through it.

When you establish that the sovereignty of the people is unlimited, you create and toss at random into human society a degree of power which is too large in itself, and which is bound to constitute an evil, in whatever hands it is placed. Entrust it to one man, to several, to all, you will still find that it is equally an evil. . . . There are weights too heavy for the hand of man.[5]

The principle of popular sovereignty is more negative than positive, more critical than founding. It signifies essentially that no individual or group has the right to subject the body of citizens to its particular will, or, put another way, that all legitimate power must be delegated by the body of citizens. But this does not at all mean that power thus delegated can do whatever it pleases:

There is, on the contrary, a part of human existence which by necessity remains individual and independent, and which is, by right, outside any social competence. Sovereignty has only a limited and relative existence. At the point where independence and individual existence begin, the jurisdiction of sovereignty ends. If society oversteps this line, it is as guilty as the despot who has, as his only title, his exterminating sword. Society cannot exceed its competence without usurpation, nor bypass the majority without being factious. . . . Were it the whole of the nation, save the citizen whom it oppresses, it would be none the more legitimate.[6]

The dangerously false idea of unlimited popular sovereignty relies on the authority of Rousseau, whose *Social Contract,* "so often invoked in favor of liberty [was] the most formidable support for all kinds of despotism."

However, Rousseau himself "was appalled by . . . the immense social power which he had thus created, he did not know into whose hands to commit such monstrous force. . . . He declared that sovereignty could not be alienated, delegated or represented. This was equivalent to declaring, in other words, that it could not be exercised. It meant in practice destroying the principle he had just proclaimed."[7] In Constant's eyes, Rousseau himself admitted that his principle was essentially inapplicable, hence false.

As a critical description of the functioning of the idea of popular sovereignty, Constant's analysis is unassailable. However, it presents a difficulty in principle. Constant maintains that Rousseau "destroyed" the principle he had proclaimed. But how is he himself any different when he poses the "incontestable" character of popular sovereignty and simultaneously underlines that a part of human existence is by nature beyond the jurisdiction of this sovereignty? Is he not contradicting himself like Rousseau, and for the same reasons, when he says that popular sovereignty is both incontestable and essentially limited?

Popular sovereignty, as Constant understands it, cannot be only negative. The negative or critical interpretation of this sovereignty, reduced to itself, would signify only anarchy, in the strict sense of the term: no individual or group has the right to subject others to its particular will. But the concept of popular sovereignty serves not only to criticize certain governments, to show their illegitimacy; it also founds new governments, it has a positive sense. If, then, a part of human existence escapes popular sovereignty by right, it escapes the political order itself. Since the latter is founded on consent, this part of existence therefore escapes the order of consent, and returns to the rule of force. Rousseau would doubtlessly have replied that, in order to preserve liberty, Constant let the state of nature (which is the rule of force) survive, and that because he failed to reflect on the state of nature, he is incapable of surmounting it.

This objection to liberalism will develop throughout the nineteenth century. It presents a group of social and economic relationships as *natural,* escaping by right social jurisdiction or popular sovereignty, but since these relationships have not been instituted by the people's will or consent, they are consequently founded on force. One version of the socialist program will be expressed in this way: socialism is a matter of extending popular sovereignty to a domain—the social and economic, that of the firm—from which liberalism had excluded it.

Whatever the aptness of his critical description, Constant's position on the level of principles is rather thin. This is doubtless why, in the text I have just quoted, it is not principally to the *idea* of popular sovereignty that he attributes the misfortunes of the Revolution, but rather to an *image,* that of an ancient city-state (Sparta) which possessed the soul of the revolutionaries. If they became despots, in spite of their good intentions, it was not because they blindly followed the logic of the idea of popular sovereignty, but because they conceived of liberty in the ancient way, because they wanted to realize in modern France the liberty of the ancients.

It could be argued that Constant's shifting criticism simply reflects the dual allegiance of the revolutionaries—for whom popular sovereignty and ancient liberty are identical—a dual allegiance that itself reflects Rousseau's ambiguity.[8] But, depending on whether one concentrates on the idea of popular sovereignty or on the image of the ancient city-state, one will be pointed in one of two very different directions. In the former case, one will call into question an idea that liberalism must acknowledge, in one way or another; one therefore risks implicating liberalism itself, becoming a "reactionary" who believes that certain of the greatest evils of modern politics have their source in its principles. If, on the contrary, one incriminates the image of the ancient city-state, one is led to perceive these evils as alien to the foundation of this politics, to define them as anachronisms. Constant's extraordinary critical capacity regarding the Revolution and the Empire stems from the fact that he can pursue simultaneously these two lines of criticism. He did not manage to choose between them, but he definitely accentuated the latter—failing which he would have ceased to be a liberal.[9]

How does Constant present the contrast between the "liberty of the ancients" and the "liberty of the moderns"? Here is his characterization of the former:

> In the republics of antiquity, the exiguous scale of the territory meant that each citizen had, politically speaking, a great personal importance. The exercise of the rights of citizenship represented the occupation and, so to speak, the amusement of all. The whole people contributed to the making of the laws, pronounced judgments, decided on war and peace. The share of the individual in national sovereignty was by no means, as it is now, an abstract supposition. The will of each individual had a real influence; the exercise of that will was a vivid and repeated pleasure. It followed from this that the ancients were prepared for the conservation of their political importance, and of their share in the administration of the state, to renounce their private independence.
>
> This renunciation was indeed necessary; since to enable a people to enjoy the widest possible political rights, that is that each citizen may have his share in sovereignty, it is necessary to have institutions which maintain equality, prevent the increase of fortunes, proscribe distinctions, and are set in opposition to the influence of wealth, talents and even virtue. Clearly all these institutions limit liberty and endanger individual security.[10]

And here is his characterization of the latter:

> The advantage that liberty, as the ancients conceived it, brought people, was actually to belong to the ranks of the rulers; this was a real advantage, a

pleasure at the same time flattering and solid. The advantage that liberty brings people amongst the moderns is that of being represented, and of contributing to that representation by one's choice. It is undoubtedly an advantage because it is a safeguard; but the immediate pleasure is less vivid; it does not include any of the enjoyments of power; it is a pleasure of reflection, while that of the ancients was one of action. It is clear that the former is less attractive; one could not exact from men as many sacrifices to win and maintain it.

At the same time, these sacrifices would be much more painful: the progress of civilization, the commercial tendency of the age, the communication among the peoples, have infinitely multiplied and varied the means of individual happiness. To be happy, men need only to be left in perfect independence in all that concerns their occupations, their undertakings, their sphere of activity, their fantasies.

The ancients found greater satisfaction in their public existence, and fewer in their private life; consequently, when they sacrificed individual to political liberty, they sacrificed less to gain more. Almost all the pleasures of the moderns lie in their private life. The immense majority, always excluded from power, necessarily take only a very passing interest in their public existence. Consequently, in imitating the ancients, the moderns would sacrifice more to obtain less.[11]

It is clear that Constant is in no way asserting the superiority of modern principles over those of the ancients. He is simply saying that in the ancient city-state, the social and political conditions of human happiness were radically different from what they are in modern states. By refusing to make a value judgment regarding these two versions of human happiness, he necessarily condemns attempts to impose on a given social and moral state any political institutions modeled on a radically different state. Constant is not asserting, as Montesquieu had clearly suggested, that modern liberty is friendlier to man's nature than was ancient liberty, or that ancient liberty is "inhuman," or brutalizes his nature. He is simply maintaining that the application of ancient politics to the modern social state makes men suffer terribly, because it makes them live in contradiction. One cannot put into "action" a political plan based on "reflection" without inflicting unheard-of suffering on individuals.

Constant's idea of anachronism is extremely weak and extremely strong. It is weak because, if anachronism is the sole failing of ancient politics, nothing proves that this failing must last forever; nothing proves that it will never again become a reasonable politics. What contradicts our social state today will perhaps be adapted to it tomorrow if the social state changes, either spontaneously or thanks to our efforts. But what makes the idea of anachronism particularly strong is less the suggestion of history's irreversibility than the psychological analysis that supports it. The specific grandeur of ancient life rested on moral conditions that, once lost, could not return. They depended on a certain *innocence* which, by definition, could not be retrieved.

> The ancients were in the full youth of their moral life, we are in its maturity, perhaps its old age; we are always dragging behind us some sort of after-thought, which is born from experience, and which defeats enthusiasm. The first condition for enthusiasm is not to observe oneself too acutely. Yet we are so afraid of being fools, and above all of looking like fools, that we are always watching ourselves even in our most violent thoughts. The ancients had com-plete conviction in all matters; we have only a weak and fluctuating conviction about almost everything, to the inadequacy of which we seek in vain to make ourselves blind.
>
> The word illusion is to be found in no ancient language, because the word only comes into being when the thing has ceased to exist.[12]

Once man has grown accustomed to observing or reflecting on himself and life, once he has abandoned the habit of action, he can no longer find the ancients' candor. He can become proud, get worked up, even convince himself that he believes in patriotism or virtue. But the moment he sees himself as a "believer," he feels ridiculous and falls back into doubt. The most original and precious element of Constant's analysis of the Revolu-tion and the Empire lies in this exposure of the insincerity of modern passions. This insincerity explains both the extremely cruel character of the Convention's despotism and its ultimate powerlessness: "The most insignificant saint, in the most obscure of villages, successfully resisted the entire national authority arrayed in battle order against him."[13] I know of no more dazzling characteristic of this insincerity than Constant's remark on the oratorical style of Saint-Just: "Nothing is more curious to observe than the rhetoric of French demagogues. The most intelligent among them, Saint-Just, made all his speeches in short sentences, calculated to arouse tired minds. Thus while he seemed to suppose the nation capable of the most painful sacrifices, he acknowledged her, by his style, incapable even of paying attention."[14]

With Constant, Rousseau's criticism of modern man and his soul comes into the service of liberalism. If modern man is essentially divided between his independence and dependence, between his self defined by others' attention and his own introspection, if he lives in the realm of representa-tion, then the world of pure political action in which each person projected himself in the public place just as he was, naively and generously, is hence-forth inaccessible. The social and political constitution must accede to this internal division and the necessity of "reflection." The division between society and political authority which "represents" it, which is perhaps the primary source of this internal division, is henceforth its necessary expression. The law cannot be the "register of our wills" since, strictly speaking, we never truly know what we want. It can, and thus must reflect only what our diverse and even contradictory actions, tastes, and choices have already made real in society. Representation, far from founding the dogmatic construction of an absolute sovereignty, will henceforth be the expression of our doubt, our skepticism. Representative government is the institutionalization of skepticism. If institutionalized skepticism risked containing a new dogmatism, Constant did not see it. Among the liberals, Tocqueville was the first to confront it.

Because it is founded on skepticism, representative government completely accedes to the liberty of the moderns, the liberty of individuals who want to be left "in perfect independence concerning everything relating to their occupations, undertakings, sphere of activity, fantasies." And if this skepticism is to become institutionalized, it must be publicly, hence politically, defended from elements of the state or society who try to impose their particular opinion on the body of citizens. Hence representative government requires that individuals also periodically don the tunic of citizens or of ancient liberty. But the ultimate legitimacy of their political action is now public opinion, the clamor made by private opinions when joined together.

In the end, Constant's political position is that of *opposition,* his intellectual attitude *criticism,* his weapon *irony.* When all its contradictions and tensions are considered, his liberalism is that of a parliamentary orator belonging to the opposition. In the *Chambre des députés,* where all the enlightened minds of society are bound to come together, he will denounce any reactionary or revolutionary attempts to impose a deliberate, hence artificial, hence tyrannical order on a society that has within itself the principle of its own evolution. He will show that this deliberate order would be all the more oppressive since those who propose it do not really want it, cannot really want it, since as modern men they have lost the innocence and sincerity that alone would give meaning to the restoration of medieval Catholicism or the ancient city-state. His irony will reveal the internal contradiction of those reactionaries whose opinions "are stamped with opinions they believe they are refuting," who "in declaring themselves champions of earlier centuries . . . are, in spite of themselves, men of our century," who "consequently, have neither the strength of their convictions nor the hope that ensures success."[15]

Coming back to his own position, however, the eloquent orator will turn his irony against himself. He will observe that if his reactionary or revolutionary adversaries are insincere and divided in their politics, he too is insincere in his loves, uncertain and divided in his personal religion. This ironic to and fro, between public life where one delivers remarkable speeches in favor of liberty, and private life where one writes autobiographical novels saturated with bitterness, sums up the "romanticism" of Benjamin Constant. Constant provided the first expression of the spiritual movement that, from Chateaubriand to Hugo, led postrevolutionary liberalism to seek the solution to its perplexities in literary creation. For Hugo, who knew how to be laconic, romanticism is quite simply "liberalism in literature." Politically, the movement also put Rousseau's critique in the service of liberalism, while, in literary terms, it made liberal irony serve Rousseau-inspired autobiography.

CHAPTER IX

François Guizot:
The Liberalism of Government

THE VERY PURITY of Constant's liberalism obliges us to pose troubling questions. If liberalism is to remain faithful to its original inspiration, is it forever condemned to adopt its original attitude of opposition? Must it always pit the individual against power, even the power of political institutions originally founded on this individual—that is, against liberalism?

Hobbes "invented" the individual to solve the theologico-political problem, to ward off the disasters produced by the conflict between the two powers; he then founded absolutism on this doubly "polemical" individual.[1] To cope with this absolutism, Locke and (in his own way) Rousseau pushed Hobbes's approach further, and invented another individual, this time essentially pacific and even solitary. This individual became the basis of a new sovereignty—represented in Locke's case, unrepresentable in Rousseau's—supposedly capable of protecting property and liberty without despotism. After the French revolutionary experience proved that unlimited sovereignty was a great danger to liberties, Constant then set himself up against the principle and invoked instead an individual sphere radically external to and, in principle, invulnerable to this sovereignty. He did not so much base his assertion on a new interpretation of human nature or the state of nature as on an interpretation of history. Nonetheless, this individual continued to play a "polemical" or "oppositional" role. Constant preserved the first moment of liberalism, where the "natural" individual was posed against the social order, and rejected the second one, where this "natural" individual was "overcome" and in a sense repudiated so that popular sovereignty could be established. To preserve liberty, he accepted the first, negative moment of original liberalism and turned it against its second, positive or constructive one. It therefore appeared that liberalism was essentially a negative or critical political doctrine, not a positive or founding one. This would prove to be the theme of the right-wing critics who attacked liberalism in the nineteenth and twentieth centuries. As Carl Schmitt put it, "there is no *sui generis* liberal politics, there is only a liberal *critique* of politics."[2]

This criticism would be unanswerable if it could not be turned equally against the right. And Constant, we have seen, already returned it by pointing out that the enemies of liberalism are in fact purely critical or polemical, that their apparently positive references are anachronisms, that they have no principles for offering a serious and sincere opposition to liberal individualism. One can add that the leftist critics of liberalism, in particular the Marxists, also conceived of themselves explicitly as critics. They proposed no new principles to counter those of liberalism; they simply turned its own principles against it, showing that liberalism, in the form of capitalism, "contradicts itself" and hence necessarily calls for a new, noncontradictory state of society, about which one can say nothing except that in it man will be reconciled with himself and with nature.

The evolution of the nineteenth-century political mind was therefore characterized by a strange critical circle. Each of the three basic political attitudes—liberal, reactionary, revolutionary—was first defined polemically to show that the other two were either "purely critical" or else "self-critical," that is contradictory. There was, of course, an effort within each position, to found itself positively, and no longer merely critically. Within the antiliberal and antirevolutionary position one finds the "positivism" of Auguste Comte, which distinguished itself from the "retrograde school" and was opposed to it; within the socialist or revolutionary school, authors like Proudhon or later Péguy sought a substitute for the merely anticapitalist definition of socialism. And within liberalism, Guizot was certainly the author who most clearly endeavored to deliver liberalism from oppositional habits which were carrying it along.

Liberalism had long been in *opposition,* but Guizot wanted it to *govern.* He expressed the essentials of his governmental liberalism at the beginning of the 1820s, when the reaction following the assassination of the Duke de Berry threw him, paradoxically, into the opposition. The state was governed, or at least greatly influenced by, the "ultras" who wanted to reestablish the ancien régime. In Guizot's eyes, they understood nothing about the new France, though they were more irritating than truly dangerous. Seeking to reinforce their power over a society that wanted nothing to do with them, they had no idea of how to achieve their goals because they were ignorant of the "means of government" in a representative regime founded on the distinction between state and society. A striking analysis of the change that had taken place in the modern era in the relationship between power and society can be found in his volume entitled *De la peine de mort en matière politique* (1822).

The first years of the Restoration were marked by innumerable conspiracies, real or imagined, against which the government was tempted to react—and sometimes did react with the death sentence. Guizot tried to show that these violent measures were unreasonable because they could no longer serve their stated end. Social power was no longer attached to individuals or families whom it would suffice to strike down in order to safeguard the political power from threats:

> Where are they now those eminent, avowed chieftains, whom it suffices to destroy to destroy a party? Under what proper names are influence and danger now concentrated? Few men have a name, and even those who do are insignificant. Power has abandoned individuals, families; it has moved away from the homes it formerly occupied. It has spread throughout society: there it circulates rapidly, hardly visible in any specific place, but present everywhere. It attaches itself to public interests, ideas, feelings which no one person disposes of, which no one person even represents fully enough for their fate to depend for one moment on that person's. Because if these forces are hostile to power, let it search: in whose hands will it find them deposited? On which head will it strike them? There are Calvinists, members of the League, but there is no longer a Coligny or Mayenne. Today the death of an enemy is only that of a man; it neither bothers nor weakens the party he served. If power is reassured by this, it is mistaken; the danger remains the same because this man did not create it.[3]

In these conditions, the death penalty became a dangerous anachronism. However—and this is the second part of Guizot's reasoning—the weakness of the political death penalty in no way signified that political power was undergoing an intrinsic weakening in modern times. Quite the contrary: the acts of power are simply scrutinized with much more interest and anxiety than formerly. And this anxiety of society had its origin in a growth of power's own orbit:

> The bourgeois, whose affairs departed very little from his guild, whose thoughts rarely went beyond the walls of his town, now knows himself to be engaged and jeopardized in the most important matters, in the most remote deliberations. The words *raison d'état, political necessity,* which before struck him as obscure words whose authority he accepted without trying to understand their meaning, now stir up worrisome ideas and agitating feelings. He is right to be much more worried than before. The government that in former days also had its separate, higher, greater, but nevertheless special and restrained sphere, has itself become much more general, more directly and universally associated with the interests and life of all citizens. Does it need money? It calls on everyone. Does it make laws? They are for everyone. Does it have fears? Everyone can be their object. For power, there are no longer the great and the small; it is now connected with the village magistrates just as much as with the heads of state. One political power now affects people everywhere and can find motivation anywhere at all. Why be surprised that

the government's condition and the people's disposition have changed? These changes are reciprocal and correspond to each other. If power no longer holds any mysteries for society, this is because society no longer holds any for power; if authority meets minds claiming to judge it, this is because it has something to ask or do everywhere; if power is asked to legitimize its conduct, this is because it can use all its force and has a right over all citizens; if the public is getting much more involved in government, the government is also acting on quite another public, and power has grown hand in hand with liberty.[4]

This is Guizot's germinal idea: modern political development leads to the simultaneous growth of political power in society and of society's influence on power. The representative regime that he sought to establish must and can be founded only on the recognition and institutionalization of this fact. Representative power that understands its position must know how to seek, *within society,* the means of governing it. It must allow particular interests already at work in society to participate in its action. For that there is only one means: to let them participate in government. This is what he explains in a text dating from 1821 entitled *Des moyens de gouvernement et d'opposition dans l'état actuel de la France:* "If then you want to profit from all the means of government contained by particular superiorities and influences, then simply hand over a part of government to them. Do not make of power what the miser makes of gold; do not hoard it only to let it remain sterile. The art of governing consists, not in seeming to take over power, but in using all that exists."[5] Just as Guizot wanted government to consider society not as an enemy but as a partner, so he wanted to teach the liberal opposition, which wanted to represent society, not to consider power as an enemy, or even as an onerous necessity. He wanted to convince his liberal friends of the nobility of governing, to show them how the liberal idea that power serves society tended to paralyze their political action, without their even being aware of it. On this point, Guizot did not feel that he was evoking a secondary or subordinate aspect of the French political situation. What risked making France ungovernable, or condemning it to be poorly governed, was surely this liberal conviction of the essentially subordinate character of political power:

> Power is indeed blind. The people's sovereignty and the aristocracy's aversion are a subject of continual terror for it. It is much less alarmed by that other idea, much more dangerous, much more difficult to handle. (This idea is that) the government is a servant to be accepted only on two conditions: namely, that it will act very little, will be humble and reduce its responsibility. . . . It is especially to friends of the new France that it is advisable to be well acquainted with the nature and conditions of power. They have a government, the government of the revolution, to found. To succeed, something other than instruments of warfare and theories of opposition is needed.[6]

The idea of the essentially subordinate character of political power under-estimates the irresistible dynamic of the relationship between state and civil society, a dynamic that denies that nonintervention (*laissez faire, laissez passez*) can be the maxim of government:

> I know as well as anybody about the deplorable and the puerile in the mania to govern everything. I am well aware of the latitude that must be given to commerce, industry, and the deployment of individual activities and social forces, and of just how much authority ruins and upsets many things when it touches them in an untimely way. . . . But, having said that, the question still remains unanswered because the maxim, *laissez faire, laissez passer,* is one of those vague axioms, true or false, depending on how it is applied, which informs but gives no guidance. M. Turgot professed it more than anyone; and, in his brief administration, he was the minister who handed down the greatest number of rulings and ministerial orders, was in touch with the greatest number of interests, and made the most frequent use of authority. He had no choice, it will be said; M. Turgot used authority precisely to abolish all these troubles, all these irksome interventions of authority itself. Do you think, then, that such necessity will ever be lacking under the rule of a perceptive power, and that, if it wants the good, it will find no occasions to exercise its salutary activity? The failing of things human is too deep to be exhausted in this way. The more society is perfected, the more it will aspire to new perfections. Could it be that you regard public power as uniquely dedicated to repressing, punishing wrongdoing, never as taking the initiative for the good? What a fanciful pretention it is to mutilate power in its relations with society, to arm it on the one hand by paralyzing it on the other! Think again, power will not consent to this, and society itself will not allow it to do so. When its government suits society, when society feels that it is living within its government, when government is truly society's interpreter and leader . . . then society will call on the government for the good it is seeking and for the protection against the evil it fears; it solicits government's action instead of fleeing from it.[7]

Thus, even if the government did not wish to intervene in social life, it would be compelled to do so by society itself. Guizot was certainly one of the first authors to have perceived that, contrary to the original liberal idea, the notion of representative government and the distinction between the state and civil society were weighed down with a considerable exten-sion of the state's power over civil society. This extension had its source less in power's despotic proclivities than in "social demand," as we say today. And if the liberal in Guizot looked on this development with favor, it is because the growing action of government on society signified simul-taneously a growth in the power of society itself. The means of power for government are above all in society. Every new activity of power does not cause government to abandon its representative role, since it should always be discovering in society the "superiorities" and "influences" that spontaneously form there, in order to make them truly "public." Government must expose them fully, so as to give them all the exercise to which, as superiorities, they are entitled. This double movement—the growth of government's power over society, and of society's influence on power—is not contradictory. It is only the two sides of a unique phenomenon, both social and political: the access to public power of the natural aristocracies or capacities to which it belongs by right.

Such a conception of the finality of political life or social existence is not as such contrary to the intentions of the French Revolution or to the liberal project. The Revolution wanted men's positions in society to be determined by their "merit" or "talent," and no longer by their birth. The difficulty relates less to the accent Guizot puts on natural superiorities, than to the idea of power of which this accent is only the expression. In his eyes, power as such is something essentially, even emphatically, natural. It is here that Guizot, in order to found representative government and institute liberalism as its doctrine, breaks with an essential element of the liberal doctrine of political power. In our examination of Hobbes's thought, we noted that the idea of political representation linked to the distinction between state and civil society implies that one conceives of political power as artifice. It is not so much that natural inequality should be denied, but rather that its pertinence for the political institution is radically questioned. Hobbes contests the significance of natural inequality so as to establish that the political order cannot be its expression—that political power has its source in a decision, that it is artificial. Here is what Guizot has to say on the subject, his interpretation of the "state of nature":

> Take free, independent men, unfamiliar with any previous necessity for subordination to each other, united only by an interest, a common intention; take children in their games which are their business. How is power born amidst these voluntary and simple associations? To whom does it flow by its natural and unanimously recognized inclination? To the bravest, the cleverest, the one who convinces us that he is the most capable of exercising it and of satisfying the common interest, of accomplishing everyone's thought. As long as no exterior or violent cause occurs to upset the spontaneous course of things, it is the brave who command, the clever who rule. Among men left to themselves and to the laws of their nature, power accompanies and reveals superiority. In making itself recognized, it makes itself obeyed.
>
> This is the origin of power; there is no other. Between equals it would never be born. Felt and accepted superiority is the primitive and legitimate link in human societies; it is both fact and right; it is the true, the only social contract.[8]

What gave Constant's oppositional liberalism its own particular flavor was the oscillation between the authority of nature and that of history, between the individual naturally entitled to a sphere over which political or social power can have no right, and the individual as *modern* individual, that is, one necessarily attached to his "pleasures" because of the development of "commerce." The consequence of Constant's oscillation is skepticism, internal division, lost innocence, and irony. What gives a specific cast to Guizot's governmental liberalism, is the reconciliation he asserts between the evolution of history and the characteristics of human nature. No less than Constant and most of the postrevolutionary authors (liberal or not), Guizot believes in the irresistible authority of the European historical evolution, leading men toward a regime founded on civil equality and political representation. We have seen, regarding the death penalty, that for him the notion of anachronism was also an essential instrument of political analysis. However, this notion of anachronism plays a less decisive role than it does in Constant's thought. With Guizot, history's authority is one with that of nature: the historical evolution led European peoples to live in the representative regime which alone satisfies all the moral and political requisites of human nature. Ultimately, authority for Guizot is not, as for Constant, we "modern peoples" or we "modern individuals," but simply "the nature of things" or "the nature of man." Oppositional liberals misjudge nature by belittling political power, because it is natural for man to respect and desire this power; power as such is something good since it is the natural expression of "natural superiority," where fact and right coincide. If the characteristic feature of Constant is irony, directed against himself no less than others, Guizot's is the haughty assertion of oneself and one's principles. I am not saying that Guizot's well-known personal haughtiness can be inferred from his doctrine. The fact remains, however, that it is born naturally in the movement to overcome the critical or ironic posture of liberals, whom Guizot judged to be powerless and, eventually, ruinous. It is born naturally from the awareness that it is necessary to show the primacy of assertion over negation. Here are a few lines where his haughty tone makes the natural loftiness of power especially perceptible:

> What are you doing then, you who proclaim that power is only a hired servant who can be paid at a bargain rate, who must be reduced to the lowest degree, in activity as in wages? Do you not see that you misunderstand completely the dignity of its nature and its relations with all peoples? What a beautiful tribute is paid to a nation by telling it that it obeys subordinates and accepts the law of its clerks! Are nations made up of superior beings who, so as to attend freely to more sublime work, would have inferior creatures responsible for the material aspects of life under the name of government? This is an absurd and shameful theory that ignores equally fact and right, philosophy and history. Undoubtedly . . . true superiorities do not always rule the roost, and even when they

do, they do not always make legitimate use of the position. . . . Also, with institutions and laws, there must be guarantees: on the one hand against the reign of false and fragile superiorities, on the other against the corruption of the most authentic ones. But these necessities of the social condition change nothing about the nature of things. They do not prevent the fact that generally speaking power belongs to superiority, and therefore superiority is the natural and legitimate situation of power. It is not for itself, but through itself that power exists: power creates itself by its own strength, and still controls even when it is working to obtain the free assent of the men over whom it extends. . . . Constitutional power is neither better nor worse than oppressing power. In passing from despotism to liberty, nations cease to have masters, but they are not replaced by servants. They then have leaders in whose hands authority is not demeaning, and who, in accepting the necessity to act for the common good, remain heads of state.[9]

I said earlier that, after Rousseau and the French Revolution, there was no longer any political philosophy strictly speaking, since history's authority had been substituted for that of nature, placing political considerations within "philosophies of history." Guizot's thought can also be placed under a philosophy of history, it also tends to free itself since, for Guizot, the evolution of history simply leads human nature to its fulfillment. In this respect, Guizot's philosophy of history is subordinated to a political philosophy, and thus ought to be crowned by it. The ambiguity of his position on this point is revealed by the fact that Guizot did indeed write a text entitled *Philosophie politique,* but neither finished nor published it. Circumstantial motives doubtless help to explain this strange gap, but I believe that another reason was at work, an analysis of the text makes it clear.

The issue is one of sovereignty. Like Constant, Guizot criticized the idea of popular sovereignty, but he did it more radically. Constant, as we have seen, admitted in principle the sovereignty of the people, even if he wanted to limit rigorously its exercise. Guizot completely rejects the idea of a social or political seat of power, of any human depository of sovereignty, whatever it may be. He does so to such a degree that he breaks with the entire liberal tradition and Rousseau by rejecting the individual's sovereignty over himself. "It is not true," he writes, "that man is absolute master of himself, that his will is his legitimate sovereign, that at no moment, under no circumstances does anyone have right over him without his consent."[10] And again: "considered in isolation and in himself, the individual does not therefore dispose of himself arbitrarily and according to his will alone. His will is not his legitimate sovereign."[11]

Men's only conceivable sovereign is neither their will nor their consent, but the natural *rule* of their will or consent by right, reason, justice, or the moral law. Politically, this signifies that sovereignty never exists as such, that it is less the principle than the end of the political order, that it must be sought incessantly by political action. It is up to political action to bring sovereignty about in just decisions. Sovereignty has a precarious existence, almost always doubtful, always to be renewed in any case, but it is the only possible existence for it in this world. And for it to be sought, no political actor must have it attributed to him *a priori* by right, since that would constitute a usurpation: every political actor must be *constrained* to seek it. And this is how Guizot rediscovers the necessity of liberal and representative institutions, and of the separation of powers:

> This law needs to be sought; it is a difficult task to discover and practice it. But, any isolated will, any independent force is reluctant to do this work; it must be constrained to do so and constantly led to it by necessity. Let then that de facto sovereignty which must command be the result of an effort, of the confrontation of independent and equal powers capable of reciprocally imposing on each other the obligation of seeking the truth in common in order to come together in its bosom.[12]

The foundation of Guizot's political philosophy lies in his resolute rejection of the founding political role of human will, whether individual or collective. Here he breaks with the entire tradition of modern philosophy. But the distinction between the state and civil society implies the founding political role of the will: if the state is to be the instrument of society, it must have its source. This source is not in nature—since then the distinction between state and society would be without foundation—but in the sovereignty of the will. The will alone is capable of giving birth to something not in nature. Thus Guizot's radical critique of the modern deification of the human will also radically challenges the distinction between the state and civil society. He himself admits it unequivocally in the text we are considering, when he writes, "society and government are born together and coexist necessarily. They cannot be separated, even in thought. The idea and the fact of society both imply the idea and the fact of government."[13]

If then Guizot did not finish his treatise of political philosophy, it was not only because his tastes and sense of himself led him to write historical studies and essays focusing on practical politics. It was perhaps especially because his analysis of man's political nature led him to question the distinction between the state and society on which his practical politics were founded. By asserting this distinction, Guizot emphatically maintained the consistency and even the preeminence of political power—though, in his analysis of the dialectic between the two authorities, he tended to link them by a third and univocal reality, that of "natural superiorities." The fact remains that his description of the specificity of modern politics rested on a distinction that his conception of the nature of human things deprived of any foundation.

The remarkable contrast between the two great moments of Guizot's political career now becomes more intelligible. The contrast between the oppositionist of the 1820s who analyzed so subtly the new relationship between society and the government, and the member of the government of the 1840s who appeared to be blind to the growing rift between the two, simply expresses chronologically an initial internal divide between Guizot the historian and Guizot the philosopher. The necessity for electoral reform that he so obstinately rejected seemed to him not a natural development of the representative idea, but rather a residual symptom of the anarchy of the will inherited from the revolutionary period and maintained by the doctrine of oppositional liberalism. It was an arbitrary reaffirmation of the distance separating the state and society, a distance that the power of "capacities" was meant to fill in. For Guizot, representative government does not have to make this distinction its theme, nor "reflect on" the division from which it was born; on the contrary, it is government only insofar as it overcomes this distinction. The only guide to its action should be, not what society wants or seems to want, but what appears just and good to government itself, which concentrates and epitomizes the "capacities" of society.

In a word, Guizot simultaneously admitted and denied that the representative idea necessarily opens up a history, that it destines societies to change and governments to permanent reform. He admits as much when he shows that the source of revolutions is the maladjustment between political power and the real superiorities of society, and then argues that the task of representative government is to bring these superiorities to light as they are and as they change. But he contradicts this position when he assumes that the conflict between representer and represented belongs to the past, and must naturally cease now that the representative idea has produced the representative regime. He assumes that representation can escape the arbitrariness of wills, and become manageable if reason discerns "capacities." In such a regime there will still be "change," of course, but only because as Montaigne puts it, "the world is a perpetual seesaw," not because the regime's legitimacy would be determined by its ability to adapt to something "new" which would be its own justification.

Guizot believed that it was possible to "end" or "settle" the Revolution. The year 1848 marked the failure of his politics and the limits of the doctrine that inspired it. A few years earlier, Tocqueville had already detected his error.

CHAPTER X

Tocqueville: Liberalism
Confronts Democracy

Is IT POSSIBLE to "end," to "settle" the Revolution? How can political institutions appropriate for the new society be constructed? Tocqueville, like Constant and Guizot, had these questions thrust upon him. However, they now presented themselves in an entirely different light. The question of the representative regime, its foundations, organization, and functioning, lost its primordial importance. For Constant and Guizot, the problem was representation: how to guarantee in the representative that ensemble of characteristics and opinions that make up society? How to discover the "natural superiorities" concealed by society and have them participate in political power? For Tocqueville, the problem became *what is to be represented*. "Society," this "social state" taken for granted for Constant and Guizot, given by history and at the same time conforming to nature, appeared to Tocqueville to be the result of a mysterious process, absolutely new and supremely important. *Equality*, the characteristic of the new social state, is for him no longer simply a "hypothesis" used by the new regime to abolish all privilege of birth and grant equal rights to all. It is an infinitely active principle, disrupting all aspects of social and political life, all aspects of human life. The new equality is not a state, it is a process—"the growing equality of conditions"—whose outcome is very difficult to predict.

Constant and Guizot had also recognized the equalization of conditions as the axis of European history, but they thought that this process had essentially reached its end. But why would this movement which had first destroyed the aristocrats by means of kings, then the greatest king of Europe by means of the Revolution, respectfully expire at the feet of the rich, or the "capable" or the "natural superiorities"? Tocqueville, just as convinced as Constant or Guizot of the fundamentally just character of the progress of equality, did not, however, regard it with the fervor or tranquil satisfaction of either of them: confronting it, he experienced a "religious dread."[1] Social conditions today are more equal than they have ever been in any place at any time; doubtless this fact merits reflection. But why believe that we are at the end of history, or that history has finally returned to nature? Where are we heading? Added to this fear induced by the general evolution of modern society, are keen apprehensions stemming from the particular character of French political history. The manner in which equality was conquered—by a devastating revolution followed by constant coups d'état—made the French dangerously unfit for establishing and running liberal institutions: always oscillating between violent revolt and shameful submission, they only knew how to disdain power, powerless as they were to control it.

In short, Constant and Guizot *knew* the society in which they lived; Tocqueville did not. To discover it, to discover *the nature of democracy*, he made his trip to America in 1831–32. For it was in the United States that democracy seemed to have reached its "natural limits."[2] The particularity of American democracy can be summed up in a few words: Americans are "born equal instead of becoming so."[3] Consequently democratic equality had created political institutions there that were suited to it and had proved their flexibility and stability. Born in the New England townships, the democratic principle now animated a vast and prosperous nation. What in France appeared to be a convulsive social movement appeared in the United States as a harmonious ensemble of mores and institutions.

How can democracy show itself in two such contrasting appearances? Tocqueville answers that, in the first place, it is a social state defined by equality of conditions, not an ensemble of political institutions. And from the same social state, Tocqueville says, people can draw political consequences that are *"immensely"* different.[4] Simultaneously, what observing the United States taught him was that the equality of conditions is the "creative principle" at the source of all American social and political realities, that this social state exercises an "immense influence" on all aspects of American life.[5] Tocqueville said that people can draw "prodigiously" different consequences from the same social state, yet this social state has a "prodigious influence" on all aspects of life, and in particular on political institutions. This seeming contradiction disappears, however, if we consider that, on the one hand, the democratic social state rigorously determines what political institutions *cannot* be—they cannot be aristocratic—and that, on the other hand, it leaves to the people's prudence whether they become despotic or free. Tocqueville contends that democracy is defined first by a social state, but he is not suggesting that it is essentially a social "infrastructure" distinct from a political "superstructure." He is defining the negative moment of democracy: the refusal or exclusion of aristocracy and the inequality of conditions.

In France, democracy had to repudiate or actually destroy aristocracy. It was not the same in the United States since, as Tocqueville emphasizes, Americans are "born equal instead of becoming so." That is true. But it is not necessary for an aristocracy to be present in order to repudiate its principle or idea. To reject the aristocratic principle is to assert the contrary principle of popular sovereignty. But according to Tocqueville, democracy in America becomes completely intelligible if one grasps it in the light of this latter principle, if one understands that all aspects of life there depend on what he calls "the dogma of the sovereignty of the people":

> In the United States the dogma of the sovereignty of the people is not an isolated doctrine, bearing no relation to the people's habits and prevailing ideas; on the contrary, one should see it as the last link in a chain of opinions which binds around the whole Anglo-American world. Providence has given each individual the amount of reason necessary for him to look after himself in matters of his own exclusive concern. This is the great maxim on which civil and political society in the United States rests; the father of a family applies it to his children, a master to his servants, a township to those under its adminis- tration, a province to the townships, a state to the provinces, and the Union to the states. Extended to the nation as a whole, it becomes the dogma of the sovereignty of the people.
>
> Thus in the United States the creative principle underlying the republic is the same as that which controls the greater part of human actions.[6]

Thus Tocqueville discovered in the United States that democracy is above all a social state, and also that it is essentially the political dogma of popular sovereignty. There is no contradiction between the "social" and "political" definitions of democracy; they say the same thing in two differ- ent ways. Saying that the social state is democratic means that no citizen is obliged to obey any other citizen—except, of course, when the latter is the agent of popular sovereignty—and even means that no citizen "depends" on another. To say that popular sovereignty reigns means that each person obeys only himself or his representative. The social state defines the nega- tive moment of democracy, the people's sovereignty defines its positive one. Such an analysis has considerable consequences for the interpretation of modern societies. It implies that the distinction between civil society and the political institution is not fundamental; both are only what they are, and are distinguished only to accomplish a common project. This project, in itself, is neither social nor political: it includes "the greater part of human actions." The sight of democracy in America thus leads Tocqueville to question the founding categories of the liberal doctrine.

Tocqueville's idea of democracy focuses essentially on something that belongs to neither the civil nor the political order, but is earlier and more fundamental. It is a particular type of relationship among men that is defined, paradoxically, by the absence of relationship. Here is what he writes about the "extreme outcome" of democracy:

> It is in the West that one can see democracy in its most extreme form. In these states, in some sense improvisations of fortune, the inhabitants have arrived

only yesterday in the land where they dwell. They hardly know one another, and each man is ignorant of his nearest neighbor's history. So in that part of the American continent the population escapes the influence not only of great names and great wealth but also of the natural aristocracy of education and probity. . . . There are inhabitants already in the new states of the West, but not as yet a society.[7]

The important word here is *influence*. Ever since men have lived in society, these societies have been held together only through influence, by the effect that men have on each other. The keener and more diverse this influence, the more civilized the society and the more man develops his faculties. But because democracy wants to establish itself on equal individuals who do not command each other or even influence each other—every influence tending naturally toward commandment—it separates men from each other, putting them alongside each other without establishing a common link. Democracy tends to dissolve society.

This fear was quite widespread at the beginning of the nineteenth century in France, particularly in the aristocratic milieu from which Tocqueville came. The liberals were less sensitive than the reactionaries to this danger. Like Constant and Montesquieu they thought that trade combined with freedom of the press would ensure sufficient relations of interests and opinions among men for social consistency to be preserved. Or, like Guizot, they thought that the end of aristocratic privileges would allow inequalities or natural "superiorities" enough latitude to assert themselves, and hence to bind society together. The originality of Tocqueville's position stems from the fact that he accepted and even radicalized the reactionary diagnosis, and yet remained just as liberal as Constant and much more so than Guizot. The perceptions of these two parties were one-sided because both confused the two moments of democracy that Tocqueville, in comparing the United States and France, was led to distinguish rigorously. The reactionaries saw only the negative moment of the individual separated from other individuals; the liberals saw only the positive moment of the individual deciding freely what his link with others would be.

Inasmuch as men living in a democratic social state are separated from each other, each of them tends to withdraw into his private world, indifferent to his fellow citizens. These separated men live in the same society, however, and their common interests must be looked after. Consequently, one of two things will happen. Either there will be a state that oversees these common interests in the traditional manner—in which case, citizens will gladly turn over their responsibility to it, so long as it maintains civil order. (The French had fallen into the habit of having the royal administration manage their common affairs in this way: having become equal, they left this responsibility to the new central administration, with all the more docility since they had become equally weak.) Or this central state will not exist, and equal individuals will be obliged to deal with their common affairs by themselves, and to this end will leave behind their private lives. Since only free institutions can bring equal people to work together, these citizens will construct and operate such institutions. This is what happened in the United States, where the habit of self-government was born from necessity in small immigrant communities, where men were obliged to learn the art of association, invaluable to democratic peoples.

The reactionaries saw that the new equality broke up social links, and they rose up against liberty. But only liberty would make it possible to reconstitute these links, though on a new basis. Liberals understood that the new freedom and the institutions it implied were necessary to the new society founded on equality, but they did not see how little this new state disposed men to liberty—indeed, how much it incited them to be content with formal freedom at the top. As happened to Guizot, they risked thinking that the new society had found its institutions only when Guizot governed in its name. As Constant rightly thought, political liberty is less necessary to man as an individual, to his security and enjoyment, than to his role as citizen. In a society where men spontaneously turn away from each other, only liberty can oblige them to come out of themselves to meet each other, to undertake common tasks, to feel that the world is more than themselves or their families. If Tocqueville so fiercely criticized administrative centralization, the scourge common to both the old and new French regime, it was not because it wronged the French as individuals. It was because centralization confirmed and confined them in their secular role as individuals avid for security and enjoyment.

To speak of an absence of relationships, or independence, or indifference, or solitude is not sufficient to characterize the life of democratic man. Such expressions are not false, but purely static, or negative. In fact, this absence of relationships nourishes a new form of relationship, just as independence gives birth to a new form of dependence, indifference to new passions, and solitude to a new gregariousness.

The equality of conditions, joined with the dogma of popular sovereignty, persuades everyone to consider himself to be his own judge of men, ideas, and things. Everyone certainly is led to this conclusion by nature. But in the case of democracy, the law adds its authority to the suggestions of nature. It even tells a person things that he would otherwise hesitate to believe completely: that he is just as good as anybody else. And it proves this by giving him as much a share as anybody else in the governing of the state. But what his heart whispers to him, and the law proclaims, the society around him incessantly denies: certain people are richer, more powerful than he, others are reputed to be wiser or more intelligent. The contradiction between social reality and the combined wishes of his heart and the law, therefore incites and nourishes a devouring passion in everyone: the passion for equality. It will never cease until social reality is made to conform with his and the law's wishes.

It should not be thought, however, that the sole source of this passion is a deliberate determination to be equal. It is not only that democratic man wants to be equal to every other man; it is also, and perhaps primarily, that he must *feel* himself to be like him. Tocqueville shows this clearly in the chapter of *Democracy in America* where he studies "how democracy modifies the relationship of servant and master." There is no more unequal relationship, it seems, than the one linking servant to master. However, while society moves from being aristocratic to becoming democratic, this relationship has a change of meaning and content. From the moment that the idea of equality is inscribed in laws and asserted by public opinion, the master as well as the servant regard their positions with different eyes. If one serves the other, it must be because of a contract, the only possible legitimacy for obedience in democracy. It may very well be considered a legal fiction, but it is through this fiction that the servant and the master regard their relationship. In this way, the "spirit" of their relationship is changed: "No matter how wealth or poverty, power or obedience, accidentally put great distances between two men, public opinion, based on the normal way of things, puts them near the common level and creates a sort of fancied equality between them, in spite of the actual inequality in their lives."[8]

In such a society, the inequalities between men therefore appear accidental. What is essential is their equality and resemblance. The dominant feeling of human resemblance has two consequences that appear to be contradictory, but actually are not. Insofar as men feel similar, each one is very sensitive to the suffering, especially the physical suffering, of others. It is easy to identify with someone who resembles us. In such a society, the feeling of compassion will take on a new importance and mores will become ever more gentle. Simultaneously, and for the same reasons, men will increasingly become strangers to each other. It is actually through their differences that they influence each other in society, forming real ties. Once differences are considered accidental, men no longer experience them as deserving recognition; the servant, for example, no longer identifies himself with his service. Differences become roles that can change in the future, or become compatible with a great variety of other roles. In such a society, individuals come out of themselves—to work, love, think, pray— only if the role can always be conceived of and experienced as reversible.

Thus, democratic society brings together men who want to be and feel themselves to be alike, but who are and know they are necessarily distinct. Their "distinction" is made apparent by their "differences," and these differences become especially perceptible through the inequalities they suggest: men are necessarily rivals or competitors. Facing this competition, democratic man has the choice between two strategies. The first is to reduce inequality by bringing himself up to the level of his competitor, and, if possible, surpassing him; this is the attitude of the American merchant, Tocqueville tells us. One merchant sees in his competitor an equal: this is why it is unacceptable to him that the competitor should be richer, more enterprising, more successful. As Montesquieu had already observed, "commerce is the profession of equals." But at the same time, the American merchant does not allow himself to be overcome by the "feeling of resemblance." He rigorously distinguishes between himself and the other merchant, and recognizes the objectivity of the market; he "accepts" the inequality between the other man and himself as accidental, of course, and destined to be overcome, but he accepts it.

The second strategy of democratic man is to let himself be overcome by the feeling of resemblance and strive to reduce the inequalities by bringing the more fortunate competitor down to his own level, or by preventing him from being more fortunate. Both of these behaviors are compatible with the democratic social state, but it is the latter that has the greater chance of being adopted. The acceptance of competition is actually a singularly fragile psychological disposition: it consists of simultaneously accepting and refusing inequality. In a democratic society, public opinion, imbued with the feeling of human resemblance, and regarding inequalities as essentially accidental, naturally leans in the direction of denying them. It naturally gives the advantage to that part of the soul that denies inequalities, even accidental ones: to regard inequalities as "essentially accidental" is already to deny them in principle.

The denial of inequalities, the feeling of resemblance, the passion for equality—where do these all lead when they are left to their own devices? And how can the distinction between myself and others, which is always liable to reemerge, be overcome? According to Tocqueville, only through a *third party,* that of a *central power* whose mission is to symbolize, guarantee, and realize equality and resemblance. This power, "being of necessity and incontestably above all the citizens, does not excite their envy, and each thinks that he is depriving his equals of all those prerogatives which he concedes to the state."[9]

The equality of conditions produces two antithetical behaviors: the taste for competition, which can go as far as "heroism" with the American merchant; and the refusal of competition, leading to a central administration to assure that privileges will not be exercised by my neighbor, a French character trait. For Tocqueville, the latter tendency is naturally stronger in a socially democratic state, and that is why he describes the former, the taste for competition, as specifically and almost bizarrely "American" and not as a generally "democratic" trait.[10] But then where is the true nature of democracy best realized: in the United States or in France? Is it administrative centralization, that common heritage of the ancien régime and the Revolution, that prevents the French from enjoying the advantages of democracy, from making the institutions of liberty function? Or is it the particularity of American history and mores that spares Americans from having to suffer the natural centralizing tendencies, consequences of the socially democratic state?

In any case, it was in America that Tocqueville observed most keenly the threat that he thought democracy posed to the greatest of freedoms, freedom of thought. This threat does not arise from the institutions, which are the most liberal in the world. It stems from the transformation that thinking itself undergoes in a democratic society. The condition of all thought is intellectual exchange, the influence or friction of minds on each other. The exercise of thought in general assumes that I consider the author I read or my interlocutor as likely to be telling the truth, and therefore capable of changing my interpretation of the world and, hence, my life. But what happens in a socially democratic state?

> When it comes to the influence of one man's mind over another's, that is necessarily very restricted in a country where the citizens have all become more or less similar, see each other at very close quarters, and since they do not recognize any signs of incontestable greatness or superiority in any of their fellows, are continually brought back to their own judgment as the most apparent and accessible test of truth. So it is not only confidence in any particular man which is destroyed. There is a general distaste for accepting any man's word as proof of anything.
>
> So each man is narrowly shut in himself, and from that basis makes the pretension to judge the world.[11]

But this refusal to listen to another does not lead to independent personal activity; it actually destroys the conditions for it. How could democratic man, weak and isolated, truly give credence to himself? He is just as good as anybody else, it is true, but everybody else is just as good as he. He has only himself to believe, but he cannot believe that he is very clever. Consequently, he trusts neither himself nor others, but only that third party which they together constitute. He trusts the masses: "The nearer men are to a common level of uniformity . . . the readier they are to trust the mass. . . . In times of equality men, being so like each other, have no confidence in others, but this same likeness leads them to place almost unlimited confidence in the judgment of the public. For they think it is not unreasonable that, all having the same means of knowledge, truth will be found on the side of the majority."[12] And Tocqueville concludes: "I know of no country in which, speaking generally, there is less independence of mind and true freedom of discussion than in America."[13] When, at the end of the second volume of *Democracy in America,* Tocqueville sketches the picture of the "new despotism" threatening democratic peoples, he combines "French" and "American" traits, administrative centralization and the unproductive power of public opinion.[14]

One trait of this "new despotism" must be emphasized: its gentleness. As we have seen, democratic man is horrified by violence; he immediately identifies with the one who suffers. This means that as the central power avoids violent and brutal measures—the democratic men who hold power will not be naturally disposed to them—it will find particularly docile citizens. Not only will it instinctively avoid brutality, it will dedicate itself spontaneously to the positive task of protecting its citizens from every occasion for obvious suffering, whether physical or moral.[15] The law's aim will be almost exclusively to decrease the occasions for obvious suffering. To speak of "gentle despotism" is perhaps inexact: one will live under the despotism of gentleness.

For Montesquieu, the principal merit of liberalism, apart from the development of trade and knowledge and the separation of powers, was the alleviation it brought to human suffering. Rousseau had already shown some apprehension on this point. Aiming directly at Montesquieu, he wrote:

> *Knowledge makes men gentle,* says that celebrated philosopher whose always profound and sometimes sublime work radiates the love of humanity on every page. He wrote in those few words and, what is rare, without ranting, what no one has ever written more soundly to the benefit of literature. It is true, knowledge makes men gentle: but gentleness which is the most amiable of virtues is also sometimes a weakness of the spirit. Virtue is not always gentle; it knows how to arm itself with severity when facing vice, it kindles indignation against crime. . . . Brutus was not a gentle man; who would have the effrontery to say that he was not virtuous? On the contrary, there are cowardly and faint-hearted souls who have neither fire nor heat, and who are gentle only through indifference to good and evil. Such is the gentleness which inspires people with the taste for literature.[16]

Rousseau's aversion to the "indifference" of modern peoples led him to two opposing attitudes. Sometimes he praised "Brutus" or the "Spartan woman" who knew how to subordinate all human feelings to the harsh demands of civic virtue; sometimes, on the contrary, he saw in the "pity" directed at physical suffering, the only feeling capable of overcoming the separation between individuals that characterizes modern society. Only pity permits us to identify ourselves with our suffering fellow man; only an active gentleness can overcome the gentleness of indifference that characterizes individualistic societies. Tocqueville observed that the democratic state and society tend naturally to be guided exclusively by such compassion.

Reacting against this tendency, as did Rousseau to Montesquieu, does Tocqueville praise "harshness" or even "cruelty"? That might be Nietzsche's choice, but not his. Not for a single moment does Tocqueville suggest that recourse to "harshness" might be a remedy for the excessive development of gentleness. Observing that this development, owing to the growing influence of equality and resemblance, risks degrading the human character, he resorts to political freedom. Only political freedom makes men come out of themselves to live in a common world, providing the wisdom for judging their virtues and their vices; only political freedom allows them to see themselves both as equals and as distinct. For Tocqueville, liberalism no longer rests on the necessary and harmonious development of equality and liberty. It sharpens its sword in the struggle for freedom, not against equality, but against the *passion* for equality. The outcome of this struggle is uncertain, since true liberty belongs to the *art* of democracy, whereas equality belongs to its *nature*.

The distinction between the nature and art of democracy is expressed empirically by the distinction between democracy as an egalitarian social state and democracy as a free political institution. It reflects the characteristic distinction of the original liberal plan in which a state of nature, egalitarian and powerless, is the basis for the artificial construction of representative government. But this distinction obliges us to reconsider the latter. In the liberal schema, the state of nature provides the motive and conditions for the construction of politics, but in so doing exhausts its role. The state of nature is the *presupposition* of political action, and is destined to be surmounted by it, by sovereignty. The spectacle of democracy led Tocqueville to reconsider the relationship between nature and art assumed by liberalism.

The dogma of popular sovereignty requires every man to obey only himself or his representative. The only legitimate condition for this obedience is that man must be absolutely independent. But as a member of society he is always involved in a network of inequalities or influences that endanger this independence. The first moment of democracy, its negative moment, therefore consists in the effort to destroy these influences so that the democratic individual can finally pronounce himself and decide freely in sovereign autonomy. The first moment of democracy is the effort to constitute a true state of nature, from which men will at last be able to constitute themselves freely in a free political body. This does not mean that democracy wants, strictly speaking, to "go back to the state of nature." It wants to found itself by achieving that state, because it wants to found itself on free and equal individuals. The natural first moment of democracy is the one when it creates the conditions for creating the only legitimate society, the conditions for its own creation.

The spectacle of democracy revealed to Tocqueville that what liberalism considered the presupposition of a legitimate political order must in fact be sought, created, constructed. The state of nature is not the beginning of man's political history, it is rather its completion or perhaps its prospect. The liberal plan, because it wants to found itself on "natural" equality, essentially opens up a history: the history of man's efforts and progress toward artificially establishing through sovereignty the "natural" equality from which he will be able to construct the legitimate political order in a fully rational or conscious way. Since nature never tires of producing inequalities, influences, and dependencies, this "first moment" never disappears. It is democracy's "nature," its *basso continuo,* since it is the condition for every social convention. This "first moment" gives democratic man the feeling of living in "history" since it makes him live within a project of which man is both the sovereign master and obedient subject.

Conclusion

This book can end with Tocqueville, not because the intellectual history of liberalism ends with him, but because he formulated the problem of liberal societies in the most extensive and profound way. That said, however, it should be noted that Tocqueville never unveils the motivating force of the irresistible historical movement that he describes so well. Here and there a remark suggests that he would attribute it to the long-term influence of "evangelical" equality. But his analysis of democracy actually leads us along another path.

The democratic project places man in a strange position. First it grants him a highly exalted sovereignty, in accordance with which he must reduce all inequalities produced by social nature to natural equality, demolishing all influences by which men act on each other. But this sovereignty is at the same time quite humble: it does not know what man will do with his recovered natural freedom. Indeed, it prefers to ignore it. If sovereignty recognized that man is free it would be obliged to recognize that it itself is only the power of a particular opinion. Man is the potential sovereign of the social world, yet he considers that, once this world is reduced to its "natural" state, it will become sovereign—that its nature will unfold in its unpredictable creative spontaneity. Thus the democratic project assumes both that man is absolutely unaware of himself, and also that he knows himself absolutely. It assumes that, somewhere in the depths of the social, man "is" absolutely, that at a moment in history, he "will be" absolutely: *homo verus et absconditus.*

As we saw with Hobbes, this democratic device was established at the origins of the liberal or modern project. In order to escape decisively from the power of the singular religious institution of the Church, one had to renounce thinking about human life in terms of its good or end, which would always be vulnerable to the Church's "trump." Since, therefore, power in the body politic can no longer be considered the power of the good that orders what it gives (the Augustinian definition of grace), man can understand himself only by creating himself.

The idea of man's self-creation characterizes the so-called Promethean ambition of modern man, who wants to be the offspring of his own works. Religious minds have unfailingly reprimanded this modern man for his "presumption," which claims to usurp divine attributes. Such presumption, however, is hardly plausible for a being whose life is, in Hobbes's words, "solitary, poor, nasty, brutish and short." In fact, the founding motive that we are trying to grasp is the contrary one. It is humble, and directed against the unbearable presumption of knowing about things in the other world, a presumption that has wrought such havoc in this one. Leviathan, after all, is the one who subjugates the "children of pride."

How then can man create himself? Certainly he has no idea of the good to guide his creation, since that would merely renew the religious situation from which he wanted to free himself, restoring the power of a "particular opinion." So he asks himself: what would I be like outside of any society or religion, simply as man? What would I be like if I had no opinion about myself? What would he do? He would be "pure nature" and would live in the "state of nature"; he would be human nature, but not yet man. To become man, this nature would have to think about or depict itself. And in this act consists the creative fiat that Hobbes placed at the origin of sovereignty as the efficient cause of the body politic.

This sovereignty's definition depended on the interpretation that each author gave to the state of nature. But its gist remained the same. By "creating" sovereignty—if he cannot create himself, he can at least create *his* sovereignty—man divides himself in two. He is both the author of that sovereignty and its subject. It expresses and reflects his nature, and simultaneously defines his humanity—whether by determining the rules of good and evil (according to Hobbes), or by creating his moral being (according to Rousseau). Man lives both in his nature and in his sovereignty. Joining together, referring back to each other, nature and sovereignty close the human circle, making it henceforth invulnerable to the superhuman claims of religion. Religion can no longer appeal to man's nature, which must ask for sovereignty's authorization. It cannot appeal to his sovereignty, which can decide nothing on its own, or can at most establish conventions authorized by its author. This division or duplicity guarantees that no end, no good, can require anything of man. What nature gives, cannot be ordered by it; what sovereignty orders, it cannot give.

Therefore, unable to create himself with his own hands, man divides himself: he makes his nature responsible for creating his sovereignty, and his sovereignty responsible for creating or recreating his nature. Presupposing the "state of nature" or "society" that must create him, he is always already created since he lives in a body politic; asserting his sovereignty through that of the state, he continues to recreate himself at each moment, since he gives orders, which are laws to his nature and to society. Since he exists only in the exchange of the representative and the represented, he truly exists only where he is not, where he supposes or presupposes himself, where he is his own author.

Man's natural desire is to bring this duplicity into unity: he wants to live where he thinks he is. He thinks of himself in nature and wants nature or society to be self-sufficient, its laws immanent. But in practice he wants laws to command as little as possible: he wants to be an ever freer individual. He then thinks of himself within the law and wants it to be self-sufficient; nothing should command except the law. But in practice he wants the fewest commands or influences in social nature: he wants to be an increasingly more equal individual. In a social mechanism where he is governed ever more exclusively by a state that governs less, man is ever less capable of receiving and giving the goods of his own nature. This is the subject of Tocqueville's fears.

The motivating force of modern history thus appears to be twofold: the natural desire to escape from the political power of revealed religion; the no less natural desire to escape the mechanism man conceived to satisfy the first desire. Even if it is plausible to suppose that the latter project naturally succeeds the former, it is difficult to discern, at each state of modern development, their respective parts; their political and social effects are indistinguishable. More precisely, the effort to escape division and overcome it only seems to deepen it. The accentuation of either nature or law necessarily weakens the other, and accordingly diminishes the resources of the body politic. Every advance of nature or the law, of society or the state, of the represented or the representative, ends by demonstrating that the division is still present and cannot be overcome. The original theme of these distinctions is to construct a law that is absolute sovereign over nature, but that must and can find its motives only in nature. Modern politics thereby makes law a more unique sovereign and nature more free, but renders both weaker, to the point that nature and the law become exclusively occupied with checking each other.

Renouncing the "pagan" idea that nature is naturally legislative, or that the good orders what it gives, the modern project envisages a rigorous separation between nature and the law that cannot be maintained, since it is contradictory, but that can always be desired. Each failure becomes a promise of success, since either nature or law, society or the state, is always there to provide what the other cannot. Rousseau's thought illustrates perfectly the singular way in which the contradictions of the project become the motive for extending it. Rousseau unveiled this impossibility when he showed that the separation between human nature and human law, thought through to the end, leads to a notion of human nature that has nothing human about it. But to show up his predecessors who presented as "natural man" a man already social or "legal," he reconstituted a hypothetical history of man's emergence from non-humanity, thus suggesting that "history" could bring forth what neither nature nor the law was capable of giving. And by defining liberty as man's true nature, by defining man as the being who gives himself laws, Rousseau incited the conviction that this apparently insoluble problem could be solved. He thereby provoked the will to construct a body politic that completely surmounts the separation between nature and law by rigorously preserving it. "Revolution" will be the political undertaking fitted to a new definition of man, demonstrating its truth through action.

For a century and a half in Europe, the nation was the political form capable of incarnating this double promise, that of "history" and that of "revolution." At times, as in Germany, the nation gave itself a "historical" or "cultural" definition which masked the division between nature and law, society and state; at times, as in France, the nation was founded by the revolutionary act. Rid of all history, the French became citizens at the moment when the general law was promulgated by national sovereignty. These two great intellectual and emotional supports of the idea of the nation have disappeared today. Communism dealt a mortal blow to the hope that European man placed in revolution. National Socialism destroyed the self-assurance of the European nation. Thus civil society and the state find themselves back in naked conflict, without protection of the king, revolution, or nation. So, turning ourselves away from prophets, we must seek the key to the European enigma in the long-neglected artisans of the eighteenth and seventeenth centuries, who at least knew that the first question is that of nature and law.

The Christian religion from which they tried to protect the polity is just as weak today as civil society and the state. But even in its present weakness, that religion still leads us to seek a separation of nature and law that it once forced us to desire. *Vis a tergo* that pushed the nations of the West toward a society without religion, it still remains sovereign in its apparent exhaustion, as if, in three centuries of "accelerating" history, nothing had happened.

FOREWORD

1. See Mark Lilla, "The Legitimacy of the Liberal Age," which appears as the introduction to his edited volume, *New French Thought: Political Philosophy* (Princeton, 1994). Whether French neo-liberalism provides a sufficient response to the conditions that have long made liberal theory and practice marginal to French philosophy and politics is a debated question: see Tony Judt, *Past Imperfect* (Berkeley and Los Angeles, 1993). pp. 293ff.

2. See Richard Tuck, *Natural Rights Theories: Their Origin and Development* (Cambridge, 1979).

3. See François Furet, *Interpreting the French Revolution,* trans. Elborg Forster (Cambridge, 1981): also *A Critical Dictionary of the French Revolution,* ed. François Furet and Mona Ozouf, trans. Arnold Goldhammer (Cambridge, Mass., 1989). For one critical perspective on this way of thinking, see Isser Woloch, "On the Latent Illiberalism of the French Revolution," *American Historical Review* 95 (December 1991): 1452–70.

4. The classic reading of Machiavelli from this point of view is Felix Gilbert, *Machiavelli and Guicciardini* (Princeton, 1965).

5. I here read Charles Taylor, *Sources of the Self* (Cambridge, Mass., 1989), as providing a somewhat different—although related—view of modern life and its relation to values than Manent does.

CHAPTER I
EUROPE AND THE THEOLOGICO-POLITICAL PROBLEM

1. The barbarian monarchies played no essential role here. Lacking intellectual expression, and with fluid institutions, they played only one role. But it was an important one: they infused an intense spirit of individual freedom into European mores.

2. Joseph de Maistre, *Du Pape* (Lyon, 1819), 2.6.

3. The Pauline axiom, as such, included the magistrates' power as well as the king's. But in a city-state, power circulated, distributing itself among numerous and often temporary incumbents: it was not incorporated in one person. It was difficult to recognize in it a reflection of the divine immutability and unicity.

4. Guizot, however, unlike Tocqueville and Marx, also endeavored to attribute a "natural" consistency to monarchy, going beyond its merely "historical function": "It has its source in his belief in the unity as well as the immutability of the rightful Sovereign, which is at the basis of the human spirit."

5. The title of *vicarius Christi,* initially shared with the king or emperor, became the exclusive property of the pope, or in any case of priests, as the Church developed the consequences of its own definition. See E. H. Kantorowicz, *The King's Two Bodies* (Princeton, 1957), chaps. 3 and 4, particularly pp. 87–93.

CHAPTER II
MACHIAVELLI AND THE FECUNDITY OF EVIL

1. The exact date of Dante's *De Monarchia* is uncertain, but was probably around 1312. Marsilius's *Defensor Pacis* dates from 1324.

2. This conception of Saint Thomas did not fail to provoke keen anxiety in certain parts of the Church. Did he not grant too much to nature? Was he not uniting dogma too closely with a simply human philosophy? Did he not have too much confidence in reason?

3. This maxim was treasured by Leo Strauss. The following pages owe a great deal to his *Thoughts on Machiavelli* (Glencoe, Ill., 1959).

4. Benjamin Constant, rough draft of the preface for the second edition of *Adolphe.* Quoted by Tzvetan Todorov in "Benjamin Constant, politique et amour," *Poétique,* no. 56 (November 1983).

5. Claude Lefort, with a completely different perspective than the one adopted here, richly develops these themes in *Le Travail de l'oeuvre: Machiavel* (Paris, 1972). See in particular part 5.

6. *The Prince,* trans. Harvey C. Mansfield, Jr. (Chicago, 1985), chap. 15.

CHAPTER III
HOBBES AND THE NEW POLITICAL ART

1. *Leviathan,* chap. 13.

2. Ibid.

3. It is in this strange manner that Hobbes formulates the "right to kill" that belongs to each person in the state of nature.

4. *Leviathan,* chap. 17.

5. Ibid., introduction. Hobbes also says "the maker" (chap. 29).

6. I have developed this point in "Le totalitarisme et le problème de la représentation politique," *Commentaire* no. 26 (1984).

7. See below, chap. 6 in this volume.

8. This argument can be summarized as follows. When we think of God, we think of Him as a being, no greater one than which can be imagined. But such a being cannot exist only in the intelligence, since this thing would then not be the greatest; this is because the thing must be greater than our conception of it. Therefore, this being, than which nothing greater can be imagined, is bound to exist. This being is God.

9. In chap. 30, "Of the Office of the Sovereign Representative," Hobbes speaks of the "general Providence" he exercises.

CHAPTER IV
LOCKE, LABOR, AND PROPERTY

1. See Hegel's *Phenomenology of Spirit of Spirit,* part 4, sec. A.

2. Nourishing oneself is obviously also a "good," but not a specifically human one like power. Hobbes kept a kind of immanent finality for human life that is removed by Locke.

3. See Locke's *Second Treatise of Civil Government,* chap. 5.

4. I have in mind only the argument's logic: when Locke names an absolutist adversary, it is never Hobbes. Designating him by name would be to invite the comparison of their doctrines. For political reasons, Locke does not want to call attention either to their differences or to what they have in common.

5. By "civil society" Locke means "political" society; he opposes "civil society" to the "state of nature," and not, as we do today, to the state, as the chief political institution. On the legislative assembly see *Second Treatise of Civil Government,* chap. 7.

6. On these points see ibid., chaps. 11–14.

7. On this point and on the problem of the executive in general, few works are more enlightening than those of Harvey C. Mansfield, Jr. See, for example, his *Taming the Prince: The Ambivalence of Modern Executive Power* (New York, 1989).

8. Precisely because they did not inherit it, but on the contrary deliberately constructed it, the Americans were much more sensitive than the Europeans to the strange character of this "monarchical" magistracy at the summit of the republic.

9. Locke specifies that this natural executive, which was "wholly" abandoned to society, is nevertheless preserved by the individual even in society, when circumstances make it impossible to appeal to judges and laws—for example, when he is attacked by a thief. See *Second Treatise of Civil Government,* 3.19.

10. Similarly, society retains executive power through prerogative.

CHAPTER V
MONTESQUIEU AND THE SEPARATION OF POWERS

1. See the final chapter of the *Second Treatise of Civil Government.*

2. *Leviathan,* chap. 8.

3. Ibid., chap. 11.

4. *The Spirit of the Laws,* trans. Thomas Nugent (New York, 1949), 1.2.

5. Ibid., 11.4 (emphasis added).

6. Ibid. (emphasis added).

7. An allusion to the jury.

8. Or at least there are always a sufficient number of citizens ready to change allegiance.

1. The extraordinary importance given to public opinion by Necker, whose personal credit alone allowed the waning monarchy to obtain financial credit, proved the exactitude of Rousseau's perception. Monarchy had ceased to exist when the king could rule neither with nor without "Monsieur Necker."

2. See Allan Bloom, "The Education of Democratic Man," *Daedalus* (Summer 1978).

3. "Discourse on the Origin and Foundation of Inequality among Men," in *The First and Second Discourses,* trans. Roger D. and Judith R. Masters (New York, 1964) (emphasis added).

4. *On the Social Contract,* ed. Roger D. Masters, trans. Judith R. Masters (New York, 1978), 4.8.

5. *Social Contract,* 3.9.

6. See *The Spirit of the Laws,* books 20 and 21.

7. Ibid., 20.20.

8. Ibid., 19.27.

9. In Montesquieu's judgment, modern monarchies tend structurally to slide toward despotism, in spite of the brake of customs.

10. *Social Contract,* 3.15.

11. Undoubtedly Rousseau's attitude is based upon a certain insincerity, an insincerity that moreover will be quite frequent among the "reactionary" critics of liberalism. Liberal society is denigrated when it is contrasted with the supposed or real grandeur of the Greek city-state, or of feudality, or of the monarchy, but when the time comes to pass to practical measures, it is hastily made clear that there is no question of going back to the Greek city-state, or to feudality, or to monarchy.

12. "Discourse on Political Economy," *On the Social Contract,* p. 222.

13. *Social Contract,* 2.7.

14. There is no point in arguing that this is true only according to the *Second Discourse,* and no longer true according to the *Social Contract.* The final note in book 1 of the latter confirms *in extremis* the doctrine of the *Discourse,* as does the note from book 4 of *Emile.*

15. The idea of "philosophy" is inseparable from the idea of "nature." Once the latter is dismissed, man certainly continues to think, since it is in his nature to do so; but this thought is something other than philosophy, even if it continues to nourish itself with philosophy's original insights.

1. See my note on Burke in *Les libéraux,* 2 vols. (Paris, 1986), 2:9ff.

CHAPTER VIII
BENJAMIN CONSTANT AND THE LIBERALISM OF OPPOSITION

1. Cited by Marcel Gauchet in his "Préface aux écrits politiques de Benjamin Constant," in *De la liberté chez les Modernes* (Paris, 1980), p. 31.
2. Ibid., p. 591.
3. Quoted by Chateaubriand in *Memoires d'outre-tombe*, 9.4.
4. *Principles of Politics (Applicable to All Representative Governments)*, in *Benjamin Constant: Political Writings,* ed. and trans. Biancamaria Fontana (Cambridge, 1988), p. 175.
5. Ibid.
6. Ibid., p. 177.
7. Ibid., pp. 177–78.
8. See above, chap. 6 in this volume.
9. The difficulty facing Constant is of pressing interest for us, since totalitarianism poses the same problem that the terrorist phase of the Revolution posed for him. In other words, is totalitarianism the consequence of modern principles pushed to their limit, or on the contrary, of the return, in a guise and in modern circumstances, of "archaic" domination in its most extreme form?
10. *The Spirit of Conquest and Usurpation (and Their Relation to European Civilization)* in *Benjamin Constant: Political Writings,* p. 102.
11. Ibid., p. 104.
12. Ibid., pp. 104–5.
13. Ibid., p. 109.
14. *The Liberty of the Ancients Compared with That of the Moderns,* in *Benjamin Constant: Political Writings,* p. 320n.
15. Gauchet, "Préface," p. 605.

CHAPTER IX
FRANÇOIS GUIZOT: THE LIBERALISM OF GOVERNMENT

1. The Hobbesian individual departs from both the Greek understanding of nature and the Christian understanding of grace. See above, chap. 3 in this volume.
2. Carl Schmitt, *La Notion de politique* (Paris, 1972), p. 117.
3. *De la peine de la mort en matière politique* (Paris, 1882), p. 11.
4. Ibid., pp. 84–86.
5. *Des moyens de gouvernement et d'opposition dans l'état actuel de la France* (Paris, 1821), p. 271.
6. Ibid., pp. 162–63.
7. Ibid., pp. 172–74.
8. Ibid., pp. 163–64.
9. Ibid., pp. 166–68.
10. "Philosophie politique: de la souveraineté," in *Histoire de la civilisation en Europe,* ed. Pierre Rosanvallon (Paris, 1985), p. 366.
11. Ibid., p. 367.

12. Ibid., p. 343.
13. Ibid., p. 333.

CHAPTER X
TOCQUEVILLE: LIBERALISM CONFRONTS DEMOCRACY

1. *Democracy in America,* ed. J. P. Mayer and Max Lerner, trans. George Lawrence (New York, 1966), p. 6.
2. Ibid., p. 3.
3. Ibid., p. 480.
4. Ibid., p. 50.
5. Ibid., p. 3.
6. Ibid., p. 364.
7. Ibid., pp. 47–48.
8. Ibid., p. 552.
9. Ibid., p. 649.
10. Ibid., chap. 10.
11. Ibid. p. 394.
12. Ibid., pp. 399–400.
13. Ibid., p. 235.
14. Ibid., pp. 665–69.
15. "Why should it not entirely relieve them from the trouble of thinking and all cares of living?" Tocqueville comments (ibid.).
16. "Réponse à Bordes," in *Oeuvres complètes* (Paris, 1964), 3:72.